MW01698583

A MULTI-SENSORY READING METHODOLOGY

Syllable Division Teacher Guide

Prepared by:

Jeanne M. Jeup
IMSE Founder

The Institute for Multi-Sensory Education

2000 Town Center, Suite 2000
Southfield, MI 48075
Phone 800-646-9788 • Fax 248-735-2927

E-mail: info@imse.com   Web: www.imse.com

0425-01

Sometimes syllable division can be tricky, and words may be approached in more than one way. A written word and a spoken word aren't always divided in the same place. Particularly when working with concepts such as complex vowel sounds, consonant blends, prefixes, suffixes, and Greek bases, there may be more than one way to place a syllable wall that allows students to correctly identify a word. *Remember that the goal is for students to be able to read the word.*

Table of Contents

Syllable Division 1
Syllable Pattern 1: VC/CV Compound Words with Closed/Closed Syllables 3
Syllable Pattern 1: VC/CV Two-Syllable Closed and Open 5
Syllable Pattern 2: V/CV Two-Syllable Closed and Open 9
Two-Consonant Beginning R Blends 12
Two-Consonant Beginning L Blends 15
Two-Consonant Beginning S Blends 17
Ending T Blends 18
Ending L Blends 22
Remaining Ending Blends 23
Two-Syllable Words — Review 25
Three-Syllable Words 30
Decoding Words with ng/nk 33
Syllable Type 3: Magic E (ME) 35
Syllable Pattern 3: VC/V 40
Y as a Vowel (/ē/ and /ī/) 44
Soft C and G 49
Decoding Words with Suffix -ed 53
Decoding Words with Suffix -s/-es 55
Syllable Type 4: Vowel Team (VT) ea 59
Syllable Type 4: Vowel Team (VT) ee 62
Syllable Type 4: Vowel Team (VT) ai 65
Syllable Type 4: Vowel Team (VT) ay 69
Syllable Type 4: Vowel Team (VT) oa 72
Syllable Type 4: Vowel Team (VT) oe 74
Decoding Words with Suffix -ing 75

Three-Consonant Blends and Blends with Digraphs . . . 79
Schwa . . . 81
Syllable Type 5: Bossy R (BR) er . . . 85
Syllable Type 5: Bossy R (BR) ir . . . 92
Syllable Type 5: Bossy R (BR) ur . . . 95
Syllable Pattern 4: (V/V) . . . 99
Syllable Type 4: Vowel Team (VT) oi (diphthong) . . . 100
Syllable Type 4: Vowel Team (VT) oy (diphthong) . . . 103
Syllable Type 4: Vowel Team (VT) ou (diphthong) . . . 106
Syllable Type 4: Vowel Team (VT) ow (diphthong) . . . 109
Syllable Type 4: Vowel Team (VT) igh . . . 112
Syllable Type 6: Consonant-le . . . 113
Syllable Type 5: Bossy R (BR) ar . . . 116
Syllable Type 5: Bossy R (BR) or . . . 120
Syllable Type 4: Vowel Team (VT) au . . . 125
Syllable Type 4: Vowel Team (VT) aw . . . 128
Y as a Vowel (/ĭ/) . . . 131
Decoding with Digraph ph . . . 134
Decoding with ch (/k/ and /sh/) . . . 136
Decoding with /o͞o/ (spelled oo and ew) . . . 139
Decoding with /o͝o/ (spelled oo and u) . . . 143
Other R-Controlled Combinations . . . 147

Syllabication Guide

1. Use *The Syllable Division Word Book* to choose appropriate words.
2. Inform (S) that this is a strategy that will help them with vocabulary and word attack skills when they encounter an unfamiliar word.

How to Divide Two-Syllable Words:

1. Find the first two vowels (vowel sounds), underline them and label each with a V.
2. Draw a line (bridge) connecting the bottom of the two Vs, ex.: V___V.
3. Underline and label the letter(s) above the bridge with a C, ex.: VCCV.
4. Have (S) find pattern and divide word into syllables.
5. Have (S) label each syllable type (Cl, O, ME, VT, BR, C-le).
6. Have (S) read each syllable, then blend together into a word.
7. Check for comprehension or refer to dictionary for meaning.

How to Divide Words with Three or More Syllables:

1. Find the first two vowels (vowel sounds), underline them, and label with a V.
2. Draw a line (bridge) connecting the bottom of the two Vs, ex. V___V.
3. Underline and label each consonant with a C above the bridge. If there are three or more consonants, some consonants go together as one consonant unit (digraphs or blends). Example: b a th t u b
   V C C V
4. Have (S) find pattern and divide word into syllables.
5. Check to see if there is another vowel that is not an *e* at the end of the word.
6. If so, cover up the letters before the second labeled vowel, find the next vowel, and label with a V.
7. With off hand still covering up to the second labeled vowel, draw a bridge connecting the bottom of the vowels.
8. Label the consonant(s) above the bridge with a C, ex. VCCV.
9. Have (S) find pattern and divide word into syllables. If there is an additional vowel that is not an *e* at the end of the word, then go back to steps 6-8. If there are no additional vowels, then continue to steps 10-12.
10. Have (S) label each syllable type (Cl, O, ME, VT, BR, C-le).
11. Have (S) read each syllable, then blend together into a word.
12. Check for comprehension or refer to dictionary for meaning. Be sure (S) can write or say a sentence using the new word.

****Remember****

If two consonants are in the middle of a word, split the word between the two consonants. (Exception: If the two consonants are a digraph [sh, ch, th], they cannot be split.) If there are three or more consonants, some letters go together as one consonant unit (look for known digraphs or blends).

Syllable Pattern 1: VC/CV

Compound Words with Closed (Cl) & Closed (Cl) Syllables

The vowel consonant/consonant vowel is the first syllable pattern to be introduced in conjunction with the open and closed syllable types. Using compound words can be a good way to bridge from monosyllabic words to multisyllabic words.

Example: Decode: bath|tub (Cl | Cl; v c | c v) Encode: b a th t u b

sunset	sun | set (Cl | Cl)	v c | c v
catfish	cat | fish (Cl | Cl)	v c | c v
upset	up | set (Cl | Cl)	v c | c v
bobcat	bob | cat (Cl | Cl)	v c | c v
cannot	can | not (Cl | Cl)	v c | c v
dishpan	dish | pan (Cl | Cl)	v c | c v
cancan	can | can (Cl | Cl)	v c | c v
sunlit	sun | lit (Cl | Cl)	v c | c v
upshot	up | shot (Cl | Cl)	v c | c v
bathtub	bath | tub (Cl | Cl)	v c | c v
bedbug	bed | bug (Cl | Cl)	v c | c v
suntan	sun | tan (Cl | Cl)	v c | c v
catnip	cat | nip (Cl | Cl)	v c | c v
pigpen	pig | pen (Cl | Cl)	v c | c v
inlet	in | let (Cl | Cl)	v c | c v
sunfish	sun | fish (Cl | Cl)	v c | c v
cashbox	cash | box (Cl | Cl)	v c | c v

Please note:
If there are more than two consonants, look for known digraphs. Underline and label them as one consonant unit.

Syllable Pattern 1: VC/CV

Compound Words with Closed (Cl) Syllables — Sentences

Have students practice reading sentences for automaticity. These can also be used for dictation.

1. The sunset is dim.
2. The man got a cod and a catfish.
3. The dishpan is in the bathtub.
4. The cat upset the catfish.
5. Set the cashbox on the ship.
6. The ship hit the inlet.
7. The pigpen has mud.
8. The bedbug bit the dog.
9. The bobcat ran.
10. The fish was a sunfish.

Syllable Pattern 1: VC/CV

Two-Syllable Words with Closed (Cl) and Open (O) Syllables

Example: Decode: c a c | t u s (Cl | Cl; v c | c v)   Encode: c a c t u s

Cl | O	las|so	v c | c v
Cl | Cl	com|bat	v c | c v
Cl | Cl	rus|tic	v c | c v
Cl | Cl	wom|bat	v c | c v
Cl | Cl	hic|cup	v c | c v
Cl | Cl	ten|nis	v c | c v
Cl | Cl	pos|sum	v c | c v
Cl | O	hel|lo	v c | c v
Cl | Cl	vel|vet	v c | c v
Cl | O	ban|jo	v c | c v
Cl | Cl	mag|net	v c | c v
Cl | O	mot|to	v c | c v
Cl | Cl	can|did	v c | c v
Cl | Cl	nap|kin	v c | c v
Cl | Cl	pic|nic	v c | c v
Cl | Cl	tab|let	v c | c v
Cl | Cl	wit|ness	v c | c v
Cl | Cl	god|dess	v c | c v
Cl | Cl	ex|pel	v c | c v
Cl | Cl	sub|mit	v c | c v
Cl | O	gus|to	v c | c v
Cl | Cl	ad|mit	v c | c v
Cl | Cl	muf|fin	v c | c v
Cl | Cl	hel|met	v c | c v
Cl | Cl	rab|bit	v c | c v
Cl | Cl	fab|ric	v c | c v

Syllable Pattern 1: VC/CV

Two-Syllable Words with Closed (Cl) and Open (O) Syllables

Example: Decode: cac|tus (Cl | Cl; v c | c v) Encode: c a c t u s

gum|bo (Cl | O; v c | c v)	cac|tus (Cl | Cl; v c | c v)	gob|lin (Cl | Cl; v c | c v)
jum|bo (Cl | O; v c | c v)	tem|po (Cl | O; v c | c v)	quin|tet* (Cl | Cl; v c | c v)
lim|bo (Cl | O; v c | c v)	hip|po (Cl | O; v c | c v)	bas|ket (Cl | Cl; v c | c v)
al|to (Cl | O; v c | c v)	com|bo (Cl | O; v c | c v)	
mas|cot (Cl | Cl; v c | c v)	dit|to (Cl | O; v c | c v)	

Please note:

*Remind students to consider qu to be one consonant unit.

Syllable Pattern 1: VC/CV

Two-Syllable Words with Closed (Cl) and Open (O) Syllables — Sentences

Have students practice reading sentences for automaticity. These can also be used for dictation.

1. Dennis has a jumbo hippo.
2. The shot upset the bobcat.
3. Melvin put the muffin in the picnic basket.
4. Maxwell will win at tennis.
5. Do not dip the napkin in the muffin mix.
6. Give the rabbit a bit of catnip.
7. The hubbub of the bash upset the lad.
8. The fabric is red velvet.
9. The goblin ran with the wombat.
10. Can you see the sunset?
11. The chap does not wish to go to the rustic hamlet.
12. The mascot is a possum.
13. Did the cop see the bandit?
14. Where was the Jello at the picnic?
15. The rabbit is in the hatbox.
16. Tom will submit the bill.
17. The quintet will go to the shop.

Syllable Pattern 1: VC/CV

Two-Syllable Words with Closed (Cl) and Open (O) Syllables — Sentences

Have students practice reading sentences for automaticity. These can also be used for dictation.

18. Did you picnic at sunset?
19. The pot of gumbo is hot.
20. The tempo of the banjo is madcap.
21. Dennis will sip on the gumbo with gusto.
22. Otto will hum to the tempo of the banjo.
23. The motto of the mascot is, "Rev up the tempo!"
24. Lasso the pig so it cannot run from the pigpen!
25. A fat hippo cannot fit in a tub.
26. The hat had velvet fabric on the top.
27. Edwin and Dennis ran to the cactus.
28. Do not tell me that mumbo jumbo.

Syllable Pattern 2: V/CV

Two-Syllable Words with Closed (Cl) and Open (O) Syllables

The second pattern that is introduced is vowel/consonant vowel. This pattern can be introduced when vc/cv is taught or independently.

Example: Decode: to/paz (O / Cl; v / c v)   Encode: t o p a z

lo/tus (O / Cl; v / c v)	bo/nus (O / Cl; v / c v)	the/sis (O / Cl; v / c v)
ze/ro (O / O; v / c v)	ro/bot (O / Cl; v / c v)	hu/mid (O / Cl; v / c v)
la/tex (O / Cl; v / c v)	to/ken (O / Cl; v / c v)	he/ro (O / O; v / c v)
u/nit (O / Cl; v / c v)	ha/lo (O / O; v / c v)	tu/nic (O / Cl; v / c v)
e/go (O / O; v / c v)	bo/gus (O / Cl; v / c v)	ho/tel (O / Cl; v / c v)
po/lo (O / O; v / c v)	fo/cus (O / Cl; v / c v)	o/mit (O / Cl; v / c v)
to/paz (O / Cl; v / c v)	o/pen (O / Cl; v / c v)	ju/do (O / O; v / c v)
ve/to (O / O; v / c v)	ba/sic (O / Cl; v / c v)	e/ven (O / Cl; v / c v)

Syllable Pattern 2: V/CV

Two-Syllable Words with Closed (Cl) and Open (O) Syllables

The second pattern that is introduced is vowel/consonant vowel. This pattern can be introduced when vc/cv is taught or independently.

Example: Decode: t o | p a z (O | Cl; v | c v)   Encode: t o p a z

a | p e x (O | Cl; v | c v)	b a | s i n (O | Cl; v | c v)	
c u | p i d (O | Cl; v | c v)	o | m e n (O | Cl; v | c v)	
i | r i s (O | Cl; v | c v)	I | r i s h (O | Cl; v | c v)	
R o | m a n (O | Cl; v | c v)	r a | v e n (O | Cl; v | c v)	
c u | b i t (O | Cl; v | c v)		

Please note:
When students are faced with the pattern VCV, they should always try V/CV first and pronounce the word. If they do not recognize the word, they should try VC/V for pronunciation.
(See page 40.)

Syllable Pattern 2: V/CV

Two-Syllable Words with Closed (Cl) and Open (O) Syllables — Sentences

Have students practice reading sentences for automaticity. These can also be used for dictation.

1. Otis will not picnic if it is humid.
2. The math quiz was too basic.
3. Otto said judo was fun.
4. Where is the math unit?
5. Why is the robot sad?
6. Did the man veto the bill?
7. When it is humid, I will get a tunic.
8. She will not open the basket.
9. Why is the raven in the bathtub?
10. The dog will go with the robot.
11. Polo is not as fun as tennis.
12. Do not put the fish in the basin.
13. Who had the jumbo token?
14. Did you put the robot in the hotel?

Two-Consonant Beginning R Blends

Consonant blends are made up of two to three graphemes. Each phoneme represented by the graphemes is heard in a blend. Consonant blends occur at the beginning or end of syllables.

Example: Decode: fres | co (Cl | O; v c | c v)   Encode: f r e s c o

dan | druff	Cl | Cl	v c | c v
grem | lin	Cl | Cl	v c | c v
kin | dred	Cl | Cl	v c | c v
trum | pet	Cl | Cl	v c | c v
trel | lis	Cl | Cl	v c | c v
pres | to	Cl | O	v c | c v
grom | met	Cl | Cl	v c | c v
grot | to	Cl | O	v c | c v
ex | press	Cl | Cl	v c | c v

grif | fin	Cl | Cl	v c | c v
hun | dred	Cl | Cl	v c | c v
trod | den	Cl | Cl	v c | c v
tan | trum	Cl | Cl	v c | c v
en | trap	Cl | Cl	v c | c v
hum | drum	Cl | Cl	v c | c v
tres | pass	Cl | Cl	v c | c v
ad | dress	Cl | Cl	v c | c v
Al | fred	Cl | Cl	v c | c v

pro | mo	O | O	v | c v
gris | kin	Cl | Cl	v c | c v
tri | pod	O | Cl	v | c v
cre | do	O | O	v | c v

Please note:
After the first two vowels are underlined and labeled, look for consonants. If there are more than two, look for known digraphs or blends to be labeled as one consonant unit. Beginning R Blends and L Blends are the most common.

Two-Consonant Beginning R Blends

Consonant blends are made up of two to three graphemes. Each phoneme represented by the graphemes is heard in a blend. Consonant blends occur at the beginning or end of syllables.

Example: Decode: fres|co (Cl | O; v c | c v)   Encode: f r e s c o

hun|tress (Cl | Cl; v c | c v)	mat|tress (Cl | Cl; v c | c v)	fran|tic (Cl | Cl; v c | c v)
lus|trum (Cl | Cl; v c | c v)	traf|fic (Cl | Cl; v c | c v)	dis|tress (Cl | Cl; v c | c v)
fres|co (Cl | O; v c | c v)	cul|prit (Cl | Cl; v c | c v)	
im|press (Cl | Cl; v c | c v)	em|press (Cl | Cl; v c | c v)	

Please note:
After the first two vowels are underlined and labeled, look for consonants. If there are more than two, look for known digraphs or blends to be labeled as one consonant unit. Beginning R Blends and L Blends are the most common.

Two-Consonant Beginning R Blends

Sentences

Have students practice reading sentences for automaticity. These can also be used for dictation.

1. Griffin had the address.
2. The frantic huntress had a tantrum.
3. The trumpet fell on the mattress.
4. I will impress Alfred.
5. The culprit got a ticket in the traffic.
6. We were in a bad traffic jam.
7. Did you tell them the address?
8. The hippo did impress Pam.

Two-Consonant Beginning L Blends

Consonant blends are made up of two to three graphemes. Each phoneme represented by the graphemes is heard in a blend. Consonant blends occur at the beginning or end of syllables.

Example: Decode: clip | clop (Cl | Cl; v c | c v) Encode: clipclop

Cl | Cl rip | plet v c | c v	Cl | Cl slap | dash v c | c v
Cl | Cl clas | sic v c | c v	Cl | Cl sub | plot v c | c v
Cl | Cl dish | cloth v c | c v	Cl | Cl com | plex v c | c v
Cl | Cl glad | ness v c | c v	Cl | Cl bob | sled v c | c v
Cl | Cl in | flux v c | c v	Cl | Cl plas | tic v c | c v
Cl | Cl plas | tid v c | c v	Cl | Cl dog | sled v c | c v
Cl | Cl plum | met v c | c v	
Cl | Cl slip | slop v c | c v	
Cl | Cl flim | flam v c | c v	

Please note:
After the first two vowels are underlined and labeled, look for consonants. If there are more than two, look for known digraphs or blends to be labeled as one consonant unit. Beginning R Blends and L Blends are the most common.

Two-Consonant Beginning L Blends

Sentences

Have students practice reading sentences for automaticity. These can also be used for dictation.

1. The trellis is plastic.
2. Where is the red dishcloth?
3. The classic trumpet is humdrum.
4. Why was Alfred on the bobsled?
5. The traffic jam was complex.
6. The hippo was frantic when he was on the dogsled.
7. The plastic box fell in the bathtub.
8. He had a classic trumpet.

Two-Consonant Beginning S Blends

Consonant blends are made up of two to three graphemes. Each phoneme represented by the graphemes is heard in a blend. Consonant blends occur at the beginning or end of syllables.

Example: Decode: mis|spell (Cl | Cl; v c | c v) Encode: m i s sp e ll

smit|ten (Cl | Cl; v c | c v)	stuc|co (Cl | O; v c | c v)	skep|tic (Cl | Cl; v c | c v)
in|step (Cl | Cl; v c | c v)	snap|shot (Cl | Cl; v c | c v)	pig|skin (Cl | Cl; v c | c v)
in|still (Cl | Cl; v c | c v)	skit|tish (Cl | Cl; v c | c v)	snap|pish (Cl | Cl; v c | c v)
mis|spell (Cl | Cl; v c | c v)	skil|let (Cl | Cl; v c | c v)	spec|trum (Cl | Cl; v c | c v)

Have students practice reading sentences for automaticity. These can also be used for dictation.

1. The cat was smitten with the catnip.
2. I will misspell it.
3. The big skillet was hot.
4. Do not be a skeptic.
5. The man had a snapshot of the dog.

Please note:
After the first two vowels are underlined and labeled, look for consonants. If there are more than two, look for known digraphs or blends to be labeled as one consonant unit. Beginning R Blends and L Blends are the most common.

Ending T Blends

Consonant blends are made up of two to three graphemes. Each phoneme represented by the graphemes is heard in a blend. Consonant blends occur at the beginning or end of syllables.

Example: Decode: s o l | v e n t (Cl | Cl; v c | c v) Encode: s o l v e n t

en|list	Cl | Cl	v c | c v
in|sist	Cl | Cl	v c | c v
tem|pest	Cl | Cl	v c | c v
con|test	Cl | Cl	v c | c v
in|vest	Cl | Cl	v c | c v
in|sult	Cl | Cl	v c | c v
in|tent	Cl | Cl	v c | c v
in|dent	Cl | Cl	v c | c v
pig|ment	Cl | Cl	v c | c v
un|rest	Cl | Cl	v c | c v
dis|gust	Cl | Cl	v c | c v
dis|trust	Cl | Cl	v c | c v
de|test	O | Cl	v | c v
el|dest	Cl | Cl	v c | c v
den|tist	Cl | Cl	v c | c v
re|lent	O | Cl	v | c v
ad|vent	Cl | Cl	v c | c v
sol|vent	Cl | Cl	v c | c v
in|fest	Cl | Cl	v c | c v
mis|trust	Cl | Cl	v c | c v
en|trust	Cl | Cl	v c | c v
con|trast	Cl | Cl	v c | c v
bom|bast	Cl | Cl	v c | c v

Please note:
After the first two vowels are underlined and labeled, look for consonants. If there are more than two, look for known digraphs or blends to be labeled as one consonant unit. Beginning R Blends and L Blends are the most common.

Ending T Blends

Consonant blends are made up of two to three graphemes. Each phoneme represented by the graphemes is heard in a blend. Consonant blends occur at the beginning or end of syllables.

Example: Decode: solvent (Cl | Cl; v c | c v) Encode: solvent

content (Cl | Cl; v c | c v)

imprint (Cl | Cl; v c | c v)

segment (Cl | Cl; v c | c v)

figment (Cl | Cl; v c | c v)

rodent (O | Cl; v | c v)

erupt (O | Cl; v | c v)

intact (Cl | Cl; v c | c v)

contact (Cl | Cl; v c | c v)

absent (Cl | Cl; v c | c v)

vestment (Cl | Cl; v c | c v)

event (O | Cl; v | c v)

fragment (Cl | Cl; v c | c v)

disrupt (Cl | Cl; v c | c v)

suspect (Cl | Cl; v c | c v)

prospect (Cl | Cl; v c | c v)

conflict (Cl | Cl; v c | c v)

district (Cl | Cl; v c | c v)

invent (Cl | Cl; v c | c v)

extent (Cl | Cl; v c | c v)

convent (Cl | Cl; v c | c v)

comment (Cl | Cl; v c | c v)

infect (Cl | Cl; v c | c v)

inflict (Cl | Cl; v c | c v)

Please note:
After the first two vowels are underlined and labeled, look for consonants. If there are more than two, look for known digraphs or blends to be labeled as one consonant unit. Beginning R Blends and L Blends are the most common.

Ending T Blends

Consonant blends are made up of two to three graphemes. Each phoneme represented by the graphemes is heard in a blend. Consonant blends occur at the beginning or end of syllables.

Example: Decode: s o l | v e n t (Cl | Cl; v c | c v) Encode: s o l v e n t

Cl | Cl in|flect v c | c v	Cl | Cl con|duct v c | c v	Cl | Cl as|pect v c | c v
Cl | Cl im|pact v c | c v	Cl | Cl in|sect v c | c v	Cl | Cl in|spect v c | c v
Cl | Cl com|pact v c | c v	Cl | Cl in|ject v c | c v	Cl | Cl ob|ject v c | c v
Cl | Cl ex|pect v c | c v	Cl | Cl con|tract v c | c v	Cl | Cl tact|less v c | c v
Cl | Cl sub|ject v c | c v	Cl | Cl dust|pan v c | c v	Cl | Cl in|duct v c | c v
O | Cl lo|cust v c | c v	O | Cl re|cast v | c v	Cl | Cl sub|tract v c | c v
Cl | Cl un|bent v c | c v	O | Cl ro|bust v c | c v	
O | Cl tri|dent v | c v		

Please note:
After the first two vowels are underlined and labeled, look for consonants. If there are more than two, look for known digraphs or blends to be labeled as one consonant unit. Beginning R Blends and L Blends are the most common.

Ending T Blends

Sentences

Have students practice reading sentences for automaticity. These can also be used for dictation.

1. Did you enlist?
2. I insist that you relax at the picnic.
3. The dentist is not a lot of fun.
4. The bedbug will infest the nest.
5. Did you win the contest?
6. Did you comment on the test?
7. Will you invent a robot?
8. The man will be absent from the job.
9. I will not relent until I win the contest.
10. The nun is in the convent.
11. The insect bit me on the leg.
12. He had a conflict with the gremlin.
13. Did you subtract in math class?
14. The district will get a bus.
15. The man will inject the shot into the ill dog.

Ending L Blends

Consonant blends are made up of two to three graphemes. Each phoneme represented by the graphemes is heard in a blend. Consonant blends occur at the beginning or end of syllables.

Example: Decode:
Cl | Cl
up|held
v c | c v

Encode: u p h e l d

Cl | Cl
with|held
v c | c v

Cl | Cl
up|held
v c | c v

Cl | Cl
milk|man
v c | c v

Cl | Cl
en|gulf
v c | c v

Cl | Cl
it|self
v c | c v

Cl | Cl
him|self
v c | c v

Cl | Cl
self|less
v c | c v

Have students practice reading sentences for automaticity. These can also be used for dictation.

1. She withheld the info from the witness.
2. Did the milkman give you fresh milk?
3. The selfless hippo will give up his muffin.
4. He did not trust himself with the complex robot.

Please note:
After the first two vowels are underlined and labeled, look for consonants. If there are more than two, look for known digraphs or blends to be labeled as one consonant unit. Beginning R Blends and L Blends are the most common.

Remaining Ending Blends

Consonant blends are made up of two to three graphemes. Each phoneme represented by the graphemes is heard in a blend. Consonant blends occur at the beginning or end of syllables.

Example: Decode: addend (Cl | Cl; v c | c v) Encode: addend

addend (Cl | Cl; v c | c v)	pumpkin (Cl | Cl; v c | c v)	mollusk (Cl | Cl; v c | c v)
windswept (Cl | Cl; v c | c v)	handstand (Cl | Cl; v c | c v)	handcuff (Cl | Cl; v c | c v)
distend (Cl | Cl; v c | c v)	impend (Cl | Cl; v c | c v)	expand (Cl | Cl; v c | c v)
standstill (Cl | Cl; v c | c v)	intend (Cl | Cl; v c | c v)	expend (Cl | Cl; v c | c v)
suspend (Cl | Cl; v c | c v)	handgrip (Cl | Cl; v c | c v)	
grandstand (Cl | Cl; v c | c v)	context (Cl | Cl; v c | c v)	
windmill (Cl | Cl; v c | c v)	muskrat (Cl | Cl; v c | c v)	

Please note:
After the first two vowels are underlined and labeled, look for consonants. If there are more than two, look for known digraphs or blends to be labeled as one consonant unit. Beginning R Blends and L Blends are the most common.

Remaining Ending Blends

Sentences

Have students practice reading sentences for automaticity. These can also be used for dictation.

1. I do not intend to go to the contest.
2. The muskrat was in the pond.
3. The traffic was at a standstill.
4. Did you see a snapshot of the pumpkin?
5. The contest was at a standstill.

Two-Syllable Words

Review of Previously Learned Concepts

Patterns:	**Types:**
1. VC/CV	1. Closed
2. V/CV	2. Open

Words contain concepts that include c-ending blends.

Cl | Cl den|tist v c | c v	Cl | Cl sub|tract v c | c v
Cl | Cl trel|lis v c | c v	Cl | Cl sus|pect v c | c v
Cl | Cl grem|lin v c | c v	Cl | Cl in|fect v c | c v
Cl | O fres|co v c | c v	Cl | Cl con|tact v c | c v
Cl | Cl bom|bast v c | c v	Cl | Cl pros|pect v c | c v
Cl | Cl dis|tract v c | c v	Cl | Cl in|flict v c | c v
Cl | Cl clas|sic v c | c v	Cl | Cl con|test v c | c v
Cl | Cl plas|tic v c | c v	Cl | Cl con|sult v c | c v

Two-Syllable Words

Review of Previously Learned Concepts

Patterns:

1. VC/CV
2. V/CV

Types:

1. Closed
2. Open

Words contain concepts that include c-ending blends.

Cl Cl fran|tic v c|c v	Cl Cl con|quest v c|c v
Cl Cl skep|tic v c|c v	Cl Cl fig|ment v c|c v
Cl Cl hand|cuff v c|c v	Cl Cl pig|ment v c|c v
Cl Cl in|sect v c|c v	Cl Cl seg|ment v c|c v
Cl Cl im|pact v c|c v	Cl Cl tran|sit v c|c v
Cl Cl dis|trict v c|c v	Cl Cl mol|lusk v c|c v
Cl Cl Al|fred v c|c v	Cl Cl non|stop v c|c v
Cl Cl em|press v c|c v	Cl Cl dis|tress v c|c v
Cl Cl ad|dress v c|c v	Cl Cl mis|print v c|c v

Two-Syllable Words

Review of Previously Learned Concepts

Patterns:	**Types:**
1. VC/CV	1. Closed
2. V/CV	2. Open

Words contain concepts that include c-ending blends.

Cl | Cl
im|press
v c | c v

Cl | Cl
in|still
v c | c v

Cl | Cl
im|plant
v c | c v

Cl | Cl
mis|step
v c | c v

Cl | Cl
im|print
v c | c v

Cl | Cl
sus|pend
v c | c v

Cl | Cl
trum|pet
v c | c v

Cl | Cl
dis|gust
v c | c v

Cl | Cl
plum|met
v c | c v

Cl | Cl
mis|spell
v c | c v

Cl | Cl
slip|slop
v c | c v

Cl | Cl
stand|still
v c | c v

Cl | Cl
hand|grip
v c | c v

Cl | Cl
in|sult
v c | c v

Cl | Cl
en|gulf
v c | c v

Cl | Cl
dis|trust
v c | c v

Cl | Cl
in|step
v c | c v

Cl | Cl
com|ment
v c | c v

Two-Syllable Words

Review of Previously Learned Concepts

Patterns:	**Types:**
1. VC/CV	1. Closed
2. V/CV	2. Open

Words contain concepts that include c-ending blends.

tan|trum (Cl | Cl; v c | c v)	en|trust (Cl | Cl; v c | c v)
dis|rupt (Cl | Cl; v c | c v)	ab|sent (Cl | Cl; v c | c v)
mis|trust (Cl | Cl; v c | c v)	kin|dred (Cl | Cl; v c | c v)
dan|druff (Cl | Cl; v c | c v)	frag|ment (Cl | Cl; v c | c v)

Two-Syllable Words

Review of Previously Learned Concepts Sentences

Have students practice reading sentences for automaticity. These can also be used for dictation.

1. Chad can fill the ad with candid info.
2. The goddess will enchant the goblin.
3. Beth will express her love at sunset.
4. The culprit at the picnic was the bandit.
5. Will Alfred get on the ship?
6. The math unit is complex.
7. Do not let an insect run up that trellis!
8. When Dustin has a tantrum, he is frantic.
9. The mastiff dug up a flip-flop.
10. Melvin does not have dandruff.
11. In math class, we subtract.
12. Put the wet poncho in the bathtub.
13. Edwin will entrust Seth to help him nab the culprit.

Three-Syllable Words

With and Without Blends

Always find the first two vowels and label. Next, label consonants and divide the first two syllables. If there is another vowel in the word that is not an "e" at the end, continue to divide the word.

Example: Decode: At|lan|tic (Cl | Cl | Cl; v c|c v c|c v) Encode: A t l a n t i c

- At|lan|tic — Cl | Cl | Cl — v c|c v c|c v
- fan|tas|tic — Cl | Cl | Cl — v c|c v c|c v
- hob|gob|lin — Cl | Cl | Cl — v c|c v c|c v
- in|sis|tent — Cl | Cl | Cl — v c|c v c|c v
- vol|ca|no — Cl | O | O — v c|c v|c v
- bom|bas|tic — Cl | Cl | Cl — v c|c v c|c v
- lem|nis|cus — Cl | Cl | Cl — v c|c v c|c v
- Wis|con|sin — Cl | Cl | Cl — v c|c v c|c v
- pal|met|to — Cl | Cl | O — v c|c v c|c v
- prog|nos|tic — Cl | Cl | Cl — v c|c v c|c v
- in|trin|sic — Cl | Cl | Cl — v c|c v c|c v
- en|camp|ment — Cl | Cl | Cl — v c|c v c|c v
- in|cum|bent — Cl | Cl | Cl — v c|c v c|c v
- al|fres|co — Cl | Cl | O — v c|c v c|c v
- ec|lec|tic — Cl | Cl | Cl — v c|c v c|c v

Please note:
After the first two vowels are underlined and labeled, look for consonants. If there are more than two, look for known digraphs or blends to be labeled as one consonant unit. Beginning R Blends and L Blends are the most common.

Three-Syllable Words

With and Without Blends

Always find the first two vowels and label. Next, label consonants and divide the first two syllables. If there is another vowel in the word that is not an "e" at the end, continue to divide the word.

Example: Decode: A t | l a n | t i c (Cl | Cl | Cl; v c | c v c | c v)   Encode: A t l a n t i c

Al | gon | quin (Cl | Cl | Cl; v c | c v c | c v)

en | chan | tress (Cl | Cl | Cl; v c | c v c | c v)

suc | cu | lent (Cl | O | Cl; v c | c v | c v)

es | pres | so (Cl | Cl | O; v c | c v c | c v)

ac | ro | bat (Cl | O | Cl; v c | c v | c v)

Please note:
After the first two vowels are underlined and labeled, look for consonants. If there are more than two, look for known digraphs or blends to be labeled as one consonant unit. Beginning R Blends and L Blends are the most common

Three-Syllable Words

Sentences

Have students practice reading sentences for automaticity. These can also be used for dictation.

1. Maxwell is fantastic at tennis.
2. We will fish for catfish in the Atlantic.
3. A mantis hid in the palmetto.
4. Elvis got a banjo at the eclectic shop.
5. Bob cannot go to Wisconsin.
6. The Algonquin people do not live by the Atlantic.
7. Willis got his banjo in Wisconsin.
8. We can picnic alfresco if the sun is out.
9. The hobgoblin was not upset.
10. I wish to sip a cup of hot espresso with a dab of nutmeg.
11. Pam is in a fantastic quintet.
12. Did you see a palmetto?
13. I am insistent that Dustin should stop his tantrum!
14. Where is the encampment?
15. The acrobat can bend and jump.
16. Can I fish in the Atlantic?
17. The best gift is an espresso.
18. Will the incumbent win?
19. The acrobat will land in the net.
20. Do not insult the frantic hobgoblin.
21. Espresso is best when fresh and hot.

Decoding Words with ng/nk

Have students practice circling the ng/nk unit that ends a syllable. Then have them split the word and read. (If circling the ng/nk unit doesn't determine the placement of the syllable wall, students can use the traditional strategy of underlining and labeling [e.g., see "mustang" below]. When underlining and labeling to divide the word, keep the entire ng/nk unit together and label it with a "v.")

Example: Decode: r i n g | l e t Encode: r ing l e t

Exception: In a word such as "mango," in which a vowel follows the "ng" combination, the /ng/ sound is spelled with the "n," and the word is divided between the "n" and the "g." The "g" can be heard as /g/ in the separate syllable. ("Mango" is divided as man/go, but we pronounce it /mang/ /gō/.)

r i n g | l e t	Cl c h i p | m u n k v c | c v	a n k | l e t
l o n g | h a n d	t r i n k | e t	b a n k | r u p t
s o n g | f e s t	F r a n k | l i n	i n k | w e l l
Cl c u f f | l i n k v c | c v	Cl i n | n i n g v c | c v	Cl u n | s u n g v c | c v
Cl m u s | t a n g v c | c v	i n k | l i n g	t h a n k | f u l
O r e | t h i n k v | c v	Cl s a n d | b a n k v c | c v	

Decoding Words with ng/nk

Words with a vowel following the "ng" combination:

Cl | O man|go v c | c v	Cl | O bin|go v c | c v	Cl | O tan|go v c | c v

Have students practice reading sentences for automaticity. These can also be used for dictation.

1. Franklin got the trinket from the pond.
2. The ringlet fell on her dress.
3. The mustang will run with the chipmunk.
4. I had an inkling that I would get an anklet.
5. Do not go bankrupt!

Syllable Type 3: Magic E (ME)

Two-Syllable Words

The Magic E jumps over one consonant and empowers the single vowel to shout its own name.

Example: Decode: ex|hale (Cl | ME; v c | c v) Encode: e x h a l e***

rep|tile (Cl | ME; v c | c v)	im|bibe (Cl | ME; v c | c v)
dis|like (Cl | ME; v c | c v)	mis|take (Cl | ME; v c | c v)
trom|bone (Cl | ME; v c | c v)	man|date (Cl | ME; v c | c v)
cas|cade (Cl | ME; v c | c v)	sub|lime (Cl | ME; v c | c v)
cup|cake (Cl | ME; v c | c v)	mun|dane (Cl | ME; v c | c v)
land|scape (Cl | ME; v c | c v)	ben|zene (Cl | ME; v c | c v)
bath|robe (Cl | ME; v c | c v)	in|hale (Cl | ME; v c | c v)
in|side (Cl | ME; v c | c v)	tad|pole (Cl | ME; v c | c v)
in|vite (Cl | ME; v c | c v)	un|safe (Cl | ME; v c | c v)

Syllable Type 3: Magic E (ME)

Two-Syllable Words

The Magic E jumps over one consonant and empowers the single vowel to shout its own name.

Example: Decode: ex|hale (Cl | ME; v c | c v) Encode: e x h a l e***

Cl | ME — es|cape — v c | c v	Cl | ME — in|vade — v c | c v
Cl | ME — dic|tate — v c | c v	Cl | ME — ex|hale — v c | c v
Cl | ME — dis|pute — v c | c v	Cl | ME — ship|shape — v c | c v
Cl | ME — pan|cake — v c | c v	Cl | ME — mem|brane — v c | c v
O | ME — cre|mate — v | c v	Cl | ME — tex|tile — v c | c v
O | ME — bu|tane — v | c v	Cl | ME — land|line — v c | c v
O | ME — e|lope — v | c v	Cl | ME — ig|nite — v c | c v
O | ME — va|cate — v | c v	Cl | ME — in|voke — v c | c v
Cl | ME — ex|treme — v c | c v	

Syllable Type 3: Magic E (ME)

Two-Syllable Words

The Magic E jumps over one consonant and empowers the single vowel to shout its own name.

Example: Decode: ex|hale (Cl | ME; v c | c v) Encode: exhale***

concrete (Cl | ME)

obese (O | ME)

stampede (Cl | ME)

exclude (Cl | ME)

cognate (Cl | ME)

debate (O | ME)

humane (O | ME)

Three-Syllable Words

infiltrate (Cl | Cl | ME)

intestate (Cl | Cl | ME)

infantile (Cl | Cl | ME)

compensate (Cl | Cl | ME)

contemplate (Cl | Cl | ME)

illustrate (Cl | Cl | ME)

amputate (Cl | O | ME)

incubate (Cl | O | ME)

Syllable Type 3: Magic E (ME)

Sentences

Have students practice reading sentences for automaticity. These can also be used for dictation.

1. Will the men invade the combat zone?
2. Melvin must not fixate on his escape plan.
3. I will vacate my home if a snake is inside!
4. The soft bathrobe is made of velvet.
5. Pete fell off his bike and hit the concrete.
6. We will hike to the cascade at the top of the slope.
7. The flat landscape will make the bike ride less complex.
8. Edwin will not elope with Jane.
9. Maxwell ate a thick pancake inside the ship.
10. Jake and Jane hope to elope and save the cost of a wedding.
11. The impact of the volcano was extreme.
12. Is a trumpet as big as a trombone?
13. Steve will take the note if you dictate it to him.
14. It is rude to exclude Dale from the club.
15. Jane will illustrate in the tablet.
16. Does a reptile like to run in the sand?

Syllable Type 3: Magic E (ME)

Sentences

Have students practice reading sentences for automaticity. These can also be used for dictation.

17. Calculate the tax on the sale of the home.
18. We will have to vacate fast if we make a mistake.
19. Put the note on the ledge.
20. Mike should check the landline.
21. Edwin must contemplate the risk of the escape.
22. Did you dictate a mistake in the note?

Syllable Pattern 3: VC/V

Two-Syllable Words

This pattern is the second choice when faced with a vowel consonant vowel pattern. It is introduced separately from the pattern V/CV.

Example: Decode: r a d | i s h (Cl | Cl; v c | v)   Encode: r a d i s h

cab|in	proj|ect	rap|id
com|ic	rel|ic	liv|id
cred|it	pol|ish	stat|ic
crit|ic	tox|ic	tim|id
viv|id	col|ic	Span|ish
fam|ish	sev|en	triv|et
pan|ic	riv|et	tep|id
rad|ish	lav|ish	ton|ic

Syllable Pattern 3: VC/V

Two-Syllable Words

This pattern is the second choice when faced with a vowel consonant vowel pattern. It is introduced separately from the pattern V/CV.

Example: Decode: rad|ish (Cl | Cl; v c | v) Encode: radish

com|et (Cl | Cl; v c | v)	lim|it (Cl | Cl; v c | v)	
lin|en (Cl | Cl; v c | v)	frol|ic (Cl | Cl; v c | v)	
men|u (Cl | O; v c | v)	vom|it (Cl | Cl; v c | v)	
Brit|ish (Cl | Cl; v c | v)	pun|ish (Cl | Cl; v c | v)	
ep|ic (Cl | Cl; v c | v)	fix|ate (Cl | ME; v c | v)	
fin|ish (Cl | Cl; v c | v)		
blem|ish (Cl | Cl; v c | v)		
Lat|in (Cl | Cl; v c | v)		

Syllable Pattern 3: VC/V

Sentences

Have students practice reading sentences for automaticity. These can also be used for dictation.

1. Gumbo is not on the menu.
2. The epic film will win the contest.
3. Robin did not finish the math project.
4. Pam had a blemish on her skin.
5. Linen is a fabric.
6. The goddess has a lavish dress.
7. Seven people in the van is the limit.
8. Kevin must polish the trumpet.
9. Will Robin get credit for her test?
10. The dog will frolic in the sand.
11. Kevin did not intend to panic.
12. Will the critic insult the comic?
13. Kevin ran from the cabin.
14. The menu is in Spanish.
15. Is ash from a volcano toxic?
16. The dress was made of a soft, linen fabric.

Syllable Pattern 3: VC/V

Sentences

Have students practice reading sentences for automaticity. These can also be used for dictation.

17. Is that man British?
18. If Steve has help, he can finish the robot project.
19. Will his mom punish him for the mistake he made?

Y as a Vowel

Y says /ē/ at the end of an open, unstressed syllable.

Example: Decode: b a | b y (O | O; v | c v) Encode: b a b y

Y says /ī/ at the end of an open, stressed syllable.

Example: Decode: J u | l y (O | O; v | c v) Encode: J u l y

(Y also says /ī/ when used with Magic E [e.g., type, Skype].)

y as /ē/		
	bod | y (Cl | O; v c | v)	plen | ty (Cl | O; v c | c v)
ba | by (O | O; v | c v)	ti | ny (O | O; v | c v)	twen | ty (Cl | O; v c | c v)
la | dy (O | O; v | c v)	stud | y (Cl | O; v c | v)	sil | ly (Cl | O; v c | c v)
cra | zy (O | O; v | c v)	emp | ty (Cl | O; v c | c v)	fif | ty (Cl | O; v c | c v)
fun | ny (Cl | O; v c | c v)	hun | gry (Cl | O; v c | c v)	po | ny (O | O; v | c v)
dad | dy (Cl | O; v c | c v)	la | dy (O | O; v | c v)	can | dy (Cl | O; v c | c v)
mom | my (Cl | O; v c | c v)	no | bod | y (O | Cl | O; v | c v c | v)	pen | ny (Cl | O; v c | c v)

Y as a Vowel

Y says /ē/ at the end of an open, unstressed syllable.

Example: Decode: b a|b y (O | O; v|c v) Encode: b a b y

Y says /ī/ at the end of an open, stressed syllable.

Example: Decode: J u|l y (O | O; v|c v) Encode: J u l y

(Y also says /ī/ when used with Magic E [e.g., type, Skype].)

hap|py	Cl | O	v c | c v
pup|py	Cl | O	v c | c v
ted|dy	Cl | O	v c | c v
ug|ly	Cl | O	v c | c v
shi|ny	O | O	v | c v
bad|ly	Cl | O	v c | c v
du|ty	O | O	v | c v
sim|ply	Cl | O	v c | c v
na|vy	O | O	v | c v
kit|ty	Cl | O	v c | c v
mud|dy	Cl | O	v c | c v
six|ty	Cl | O	v c | c v
la|zy	O | O	v | c v
jel|ly	Cl | O	v c | c v
soft|ly	Cl | O	v c | c v
skin|ny	Cl | O	v c | c v
in|stant|ly	Cl | Cl | O	v c | c v c | c v
con|stant|ly	Cl | Cl | O	v c | c v c | c v
ex|act|ly	Cl | Cl | O	v c | v c | c v
sud|den|ly	Cl | Cl | O	v c | c v c | c v
un|hap|py	Cl | Cl | O	v c | c v c | c v

Y as a Vowel

Y says /ē/ at the end of an open, unstressed syllable.

Example: Decode: ba|by (O | O; v|c v) Encode: b a b y

Y says /ī/ at the end of an open, stressed syllable.

Example: Decode: Ju|ly (O | O; v|c v) Encode: J u l y

(Y also says /ī/ when used with Magic E [e.g., type, Skype].)

	y as /ī/	
sun|ny (Cl | O; v c|c v)		sup|ply (Cl | O; v c|c v)
cop|y (Cl | O; v c|v)	de|ny (O | O; v|c v)	al|ly (Cl | O; v c|c v)
bug|gy (Cl | O; v c|c v)	re|ply (O | O)	de|fy (O | O; v|c v)
mes|sy (Cl | O; v c|c v)	re|ly (O | O; v|c v)	pig|sty (Cl | O; v c|c v)
rap|id|ly (Cl | Cl | O; v c|v c|c v)	im|ply (Cl | O; v c|c v)	oc|cu|py (Cl | O | O; v c|c v|c v)
	Ju|ly (O | O; v|c v)	sat|is|fy (Cl | Cl | O; v c|v c|c v)

Y as a Vowel

Sentences

Have students practice reading sentences for automaticity. These can also be used for dictation.

y as /ē/

1. The kite came down rapidly.
2. A messy desk is not good.
3. That empty crate does not belong to Sandy and Bobby.
4. Amy and Henry did not see the skinny kitty.
5. Her navy bike was muddy.
6. I will sing softly to the tiny baby.
7. The funny comic made us happy.
8. Jenny cannot study when she is constantly hungry.
9. Judy does not like grape jelly.
10. I hope Jimmy and Danny are not unhappy with me.
11. We instantly fell in love with the tiny puppy.
12. Help me get the shiny penny down from the shelf.
13. Did the lady hide the candy?
14. Put the buggy back when you finish with it.
15. Brandy was happy when she suddenly saw her mommy and daddy!

Y as a Vowel

Sentences

Have students practice reading sentences for automaticity. These can also be used for dictation.

y as /ī/

1. He will not deny his mistake.
2. Did Melvin send a reply to you?
3. Pam and Pete will finish the project in late July.
4. Who will supply the student with a pen and desk?
5. The pigsty stunk and was a big mess.
6. The people will occupy the plane.

Soft C and G

C says /k/ next to a, o, u, and consonants. C says /s/ next to e, i, and y.

Example: Decode: ac|cent (Cl | Cl; v c | c v) Encode: accent

G says /g/ next to a, o, u, and consonants. G says /j/ next to e, i, and y.

Example: Decode: sug|gest (Cl | Cl; v c | c v) Encode: suggest

Soft C

re|duce (O | ME)	re|cess (O | Cl)	
ac|cent (Cl | Cl)	ex|cept (Cl | Cl)	pre|cise (O | ME)
suc|cess (Cl | Cl)	pro|duce (O | ME)	ex|cess (Cl | Cl)
con|cept (Cl | Cl)	ex|cite (Cl | ME)	cen|sus (Cl | Cl)
ran|cid (Cl | Cl)	prin|cess (Cl | Cl)	dis|grace (Cl | ME)
de|cide (O | ME)	ac|cept (Cl | Cl)	spi|cy (O | O)
ec|cen|tric (Cl | Cl | Cl)	ad|vice (Cl | ME)	re|cite (O | ME)
fan|cy (Cl | O)	cy|clone* (O | ME)	
re|place (ME)	cy|press* (O | Cl)	

* The blends stay together in these Greek words.

Soft C and G

C says /k/ next to a, o, u, and consonants. C says /s/ next to e, i, and y.

Example: Decode: accent Encode: accent

G says /g/ next to a, o, u, and consonants. G says /j/ next to e, i, and y.

Example: Decode: suggest Encode: suggest

Soft G

	gently	refuge
suggest	agent	tragic
rampage	agency	pungent
frigid	digest	gigantic
digit	engage	angelic
indulgent	rigid	
magic	logic	

Soft C and G

Sentences

Have students practice reading sentences for automaticity. These can also be used for dictation.

Soft C

1. Cindy has a fancy dress like a princess.
2. I will replace the broken buggy.
3. We hid in a safe place until the cyclone was over.
4. Mike can plant the cypress next spring.
5. Help me decide where to ride my bike.
6. The produce at the stand was fresh and yummy.
7. Let me give you some advice.
8. I do not think we should rest at recess.
9. Did you grill spicy fish for the contest?

Soft G

1. Cindy had to go inside when the wind became frigid.
2. I suggest that we put the milk back on the shelf.
3. Did the magic robot help fix the broken ship?
4. Gently place the glass dish in the case.

Soft C and G

Sentences

Have students practice reading sentences for automaticity. These can also be used for dictation.

5. Did the puppy digest the bone he ate?
6. Where is the gigantic muddy hippo?
7. We could not bend the rigid strip of tin.
8. Bobby and Stan will take refuge in the cave.
9. The pungent smell made my mom sick.

Decoding Words with Suffix -ed

Have students practice circling the suffix -ed and determining what sound -ed will make based on the rules. Then have students decode the rest of the word if needed.

Suffix -ed says /id/ when the base word ends with /d/ or /t/.

Suffix -ed says /d/ when the base word ends with a voiced sound other than /d/.

Suffix -ed says /t/ when the base word ends with an unvoiced sound other than /t/.

Examples:

Decode:	/id/ land | (ed) /id/	/d/ spell (ed) /d/	/t/ rush (ed) /t/
Encode:	/id/ l a n d + (ed)	/d/ s p e ll + (ed)	/t/ r u sh + (ed)

land | (ed) /id/	fuss (ed) /t/
spell (ed) /d/	smell (ed) /d/
rush (ed) /t/	Cl hap | Cl pen (ed) /d/ (v c | c v)
dish (ed) /t/	O re | Cl lax (ed) /t/ (v | c v)
crush (ed) /t/	Cl fam | Cl ish (ed) /t/ (v c | v)
yell (ed) /d/	Cl in | Cl sult | (ed) /id/ (v c | c v)
melt | (ed) /id/	Cl dis | Cl gust | (ed) /id/ (v c | c v)

Decoding Words with Suffix -ed

Have students practice circling the suffix -ed and determining what sound -ed will make based on the rules. Then have students decode the rest of the word if needed.

Suffix -ed says /id/ when the base word ends with /d/ or /t/.

Suffix -ed says /d/ when the base word ends with a voiced sound other than /d/.

Suffix -ed says /t/ when the base word ends with an unvoiced sound other than /t/.

Examples:

Decode: /id/ land|ed (/id/) /d/ spell ed (/d/) /t/ rush ed (/t/)

Encode: /id/ l a n d + ed /d/ s p e ll + ed /t/ r u sh + ed

spilled (/d/)	buzzed (/d/)
pinched (/t/)	un|in|hab|it|ed (Cl Cl Cl Cl; v c v c c v c v; /id/)
crunched (/t/)	pro|ject|ed (O Cl; v c v; /id/)

Have students practice reading sentences for automaticity. These can also be used for dictation.

1. She landed at the base of the step.
2. He spelled it like it should be spelled.
3. The dog was relaxed when she slept.
4. The man yelled at the cat.
5. The dog smelled bad, but Steve still kept him.

Decoding Words with Suffix -s/-es

Have students practice circling the suffix -s/-es and determining its sound based on the rules. Then have students decode the rest of the word if needed.

Suffix -s says /s/ when the base word ends in an unvoiced sound.

Suffix -s says /z/ when the base word ends in a voiced sound.

Suffix -es says /iz/ when the base word ends with /ch/, /j/, /s/, /sh/, /z/, or the letter "x."

Examples:

Decode: /s/ cupcakes (Cl | ME, /s/; v c | c v) — /z/ cabins (Cl | Cl, /z/; v c | v) — /iz/ suffixes (Cl | Cl | /iz/; v c | c v)

Encode: /s/ cupcake*** + s — /z/ cabin + s — /iz/ suffix + es

-s (/s/)		
	culprits (Cl | Cl /s/; v c | c v)	acrobats (Cl | O | Cl /s/; v c | c v | c v)
cupcakes (Cl | ME /s/; v c | c v)	skillets (Cl | Cl /s/; v c | c v)	comets (Cl | Cl /s/; v c | v)
handshakes (Cl | ME /s/; v c | c v)	fragments (Cl | Cl /s/; v c | c v)	relics (Cl | Cl /s/; v c | v)
sunsets (Cl | Cl /s/; v c | c v)	comments (Cl | Cl /s/; v c | c v)	credits (Cl | Cl /s/; v c | v)
baskets (Cl | Cl /s/; v c | c v)	dentists (Cl | Cl /s/; v c | c v)	**-s (/z/)**
robots (O | Cl /s/; v | c v)	handcuffs (Cl | Cl /s/; v c | c v)	menus (Cl | O /z/; v c | v)
tunics (O | Cl /s/; v | c v)	mistakes (Cl | ME /s/; v c | c v)	landslides (Cl | ME /z/; v c | c v)

Decoding Words with Suffix -s/-es

Have students practice circling the suffix -s/-es and determining its sound based on the rules. Then have students decode the rest of the word if needed.

Suffix -s says /s/ when the base word ends in an unvoiced sound.

Suffix -s says /z/ when the base word ends in a voiced sound.

Suffix -es says /iz/ when the base word ends with /ch/, /j/, /s/, /sh/, /z/, or the letter "x."

Examples:

Decode: /s/ cupcakes (Cl | ME /s/; v c | c v) — /z/ cabins (Cl | Cl /z/; v c | v) — /iz/ suffixes (Cl | Cl | /iz/; v c | c v)

Encode: /s/ cupcake + s — /z/ cabin + s — /iz/ suffix + es

		-es (/iz/)
cabins	tadpoles	blemishes
mustangs	pumpkins	radishes
textiles	credos	batches
Algonquins	windmills	ditches
goblins	egos	princesses
bathrobes	tempos	suffixes
addends	dishpans	

Decoding Words with Suffix -s/-es

Have students practice circling the suffix -s/-es and determining its sound based on the rules. Then have students decode the rest of the word if needed.

Suffix -s says /s/ when the base word ends in an unvoiced sound.

Suffix -s says /z/ when the base word ends in a voiced sound.

Suffix -es says /iz/ when the base word ends with /ch/, /j/, /s/, /sh/, /z/, or the letter "x."

Examples:

Decode: /s/ cup|cake(s) — Cl | ME /s/ — v c | c v

/z/ cab|in(s) — Cl | Cl /z/ — v c | v

/iz/ suf|fix|(es) — Cl | Cl | /iz/ — v c | c v

Encode: /s/ c u p c a k e*** + (s)

/z/ c a b i n + (s)

/iz/ s u f f i x + (e s)

em|press|(es) — Cl | Cl | /iz/ — v c | c v

mat|tress|(es) — Cl | Cl | /iz/ — v c | c v

ad|dress|(es) — Cl | Cl | /iz/ — v c | c v

cash|box|(es) — Cl | Cl | /iz/ — v c | c v

Decoding Words with Suffix -s/-es

Sentences

Have students practice reading sentences for automaticity. These can also be used for dictation.

1. Did Brandy make cupcakes for the class?
2. I think I saw one of the menus over there.
3. The landslides were muddy and slick.
4. The tadpoles are not in the pond.
5. Who will give handshakes at the big event?
6. Hang the bathrobes by the shelf.
7. There were no napkins in the picnic baskets.
8. The acrobats did not make mistakes in the contest.
9. Jane and Melvin have the cashboxes at the game.
10. Which suffixes will we use in class today?
11. The dentists could not focus with the dogs in there.
12. Will we have the pumpkins for lunch next time?
13. The batches of cupcakes were so good!
14. The princesses had tunics and socks.
15. Did Bobby invite the robots to the stampede?
16. The culprits did not get their wishes.
17. Fragments of fabric were in the cabins.
18. The hungry lady left messy dishes in the dishpans.
19. Do goblins have blemishes on their skin?
20. Windmills cannot be made of concrete.

Syllable Type 4: Vowel Team (VT) ea

A Vowel Team (VT) is two, three, or four letters that work together to produce a vowel sound. The vowel sound may be long, short, or a diphthong (gliding monosyllabic speech sound).

Example: Decode: b e | n e a t h (O | VT; v | c v)   Encode: b e n e a t h

VT | ME meal | time v c | c v	Cl | VT en | treat v c | c v
VT | Cl mean | est v c | v	VT | Cl leaf | let v c | c v
Cl | VT mis | treat v c | c v	VT | Cl tea | pot v | c v
VT | Cl pea | nut v | c v	Cl | VT in | seam v c | c v
VT | Cl pea | cock v | c v	VT | Cl squeam | ish v | c v
VT | ME mean | while v c | c v	Cl | VT im | peach v c | c v
VT | Cl tea | cup v | c v	O | VT be | neath v | c v

Syllable Type 4: Vowel Team (VT) ea

A Vowel Team (VT) is two, three, or four letters that work together to produce a vowel sound. The vowel sound may be long, short, or a diphthong (gliding monosyllabic speech sound).

Example: Decode:
O | VT
b e | n e a t h
v | c v

Encode: b e n e a t h

VT | ME
m e a n | t i m e
v c | c v

O | VT
d e | f e a t
v | c v

O | VT
r e | p e a l
v | c v

O | VT
b e | q u e a t h
v | c v

O | VT
r e | t r e a t

VT | O
r e a l | l y
v c | c v

O | VT
r e | v e a l
v | c v

O | VT
r e | p e a t
v | c v

Cl | VT
c r a b | m e a t
v c | c v

VT | Cl
w e a k | n e s s
v c | c v

VT | Cl
t e a | p o t
v | c v

VT | ME
t e a m | m a t e
v c | c v

Syllable Type 4: Vowel Team (VT) ea

Sentences

Have students practice reading sentences for automaticity. These can also be used for dictation.

1. We will go down to the beach at mealtime.
2. Jenny yelled when the peanut fell.
3. The shop is not open, so in the meantime we can plan the meal.
4. Alvin the chipmunk can eat seven peanuts.
5. The team had to retreat from the combat zone.
6. Do you think Maxwell will defeat Brandy in the tennis match?
7. Do not clean the teapot with bleach.
8. The inseam is too long.
9. Dean will bequeath his home to his wife.
10. Do not repeat gossip.
11. Will the beast reveal his plot to steal the cupcakes?
12. The cat will squeal and hide beneath the bed.
13. I really love fresh crabmeat from the sea.

Syllable Type 4: Vowel Team (VT) ee

A Vowel Team (VT) is two, three, or four letters that work together to produce a vowel sound. The vowel sound may be long, short, or a diphthong (gliding monosyllabic speech sound).

Example: Decode: in|deed (Cl | VT; v c | c v) Encode: indeed

dis|creet (Cl | VT; v c | c v)	chim|pan|zee (Cl | Cl | VT; v c | c v c | c v)
ex|ceed (Cl | VT; v c | c v)	deep|ly (VT | O; v c | c v)
in|deed (Cl | VT; v c | c v)	tof|fee (Cl | VT; v c | c v)
fif|teen (Cl | VT; v c | c v)	can|teen (Cl | VT; v c | c v)
six|teen (Cl | VT; v c | c v)	Hal|lo|ween (Cl | O | VT; v c | c v | c v)
cof|fee (Cl | VT; v c | c v)	week|end (VT | Cl; v c | v)
ab|sen|tee (Cl | Cl | VT; v c | c v c | c v)	en|lis|tee (Cl | Cl | VT; v c | c v c | c v)
am|pu|tee (Cl | O | VT; v c | c v | c v)	

Syllable Type 4: Vowel Team (VT) ee

A Vowel Team (VT) is two, three, or four letters that work together to produce a vowel sound. The vowel sound may be long, short, or a diphthong (gliding monosyllabic speech sound).

Example: Decode: in|deed (Cl | VT; v c | c v) Encode: i n d e e d

feed|back
VT | Cl
v c | c v

sea|weed
VT | VT
v | c v

suc|ceed
Cl | VT
v c | c v

sweep|stake
VT | ME
v c | c v

bee|hive
VT | ME
v | c v

re|deem
O | VT
v | c v

tree|top
VT | Cl
v | c v

sweet|ness
VT | Cl
v c | c v

sev|en|teen
Cl | Cl | VT
v c | v c | c v

flax|seed
Cl | VT
v c | c v

bee|line
VT | ME
v | c v

seed|ling
VT
v c | c v

bed|sheet
Cl | VT
v c | c v

pro|ceed
O | VT
v | c v

Syllable Type 4: Vowel Team (VT) ee

Sentences

Have students practice reading sentences for automaticity. These can also be used for dictation.

1. Fill the canteen so that you can drink while you hike.
2. When Dustin put his hand inside the beehive, he got stung.
3. Be discreet when you sneak up on the hobgoblin.
4. Maxwell is indeed a tennis pro.
5. Jenny put her coffee in the canteen.
6. Alvin made a beeline to the stove.
7. Chimpanzees should not drink coffee.
8. The queen will provide feedback on the rule.
9. Do chimpanzees eat meat?
10. Cathy saw fifteen bedsheets on the shelf.
11. Toffee candy is yummy!
12. When will Brent redeem his token for the prize?

Syllable Type 4: Vowel Team (VT) ai

A Vowel Team (VT) is two, three, or four letters that work together to produce a vowel sound. The vowel sound may be long, short, or a diphthong (gliding monosyllabic speech sound).

Example: Decode: Cl | VT — e x | pl a i n — v c | c v   Encode: e x p l a i n

VT | O	m a i n | l y	v c | c v
VT | Cl	m a i l | b o x	v c | c v
VT | O	f a i n t | l y	v c | c v
Cl | VT	a b | s t a i n	v c | c v
VT | Cl	b a i | l i f f	v | c v
Cl | VT	b l a c k | m a i l	v c | c v
Cl | VT	b o b | t a i l	v c | c v
VT | Cl	f a i t h | f u l	v c | c v
VT | Cl	r a i n | d r o p	v c | c v
O | VT	d e | t a i l	v | c v
Cl | VT	d i s | d a i n	v c | c v
O | VT	e | m a i l	v | c v
Cl | VT	e n | t a i l	v c | c v
Cl | VT	e x | p l a i n	v c | c v
Cl | VT	h a n d | r a i l	v c | c v
VT | Cl	m a i l | m a n	v c | c v

Syllable Type 4: Vowel Team (VT) ai

A Vowel Team (VT) is two, three, or four letters that work together to produce a vowel sound. The vowel sound may be long, short, or a diphthong (gliding monosyllabic speech sound).

Example: Decode: ex|plain (Cl | VT; v c | c v) Encode: explain

- mis|laid (Cl | VT; v c | c v)
- main|land (VT | Cl; v c | c v)
- pain|ful (VT | Cl; v c | c v)
- pro|claim (O | VT; v | c v)
- re|claim (O | VT; v | c v)
- re|main (O | VT; v | c v)
- re|tain (O | VT; v | c v)
- sus|tain (Cl | VT; v c | c v)
- dain|ty (VT | O; v c | c v)
- tail|gate (VT | ME; v c | c v)
- vain|est (VT | Cl; v c | v)
- do|main (O | VT; v | c v)
- paint|brush (VT | Cl; v c | c v)
- pre|vail (O | VT; v | c v)
- de|tain (O | VT; v | c v)
- re|frain (O | VT; v | c v)

Syllable Type 4: Vowel Team (VT) ai

A Vowel Team (VT) is two, three, or four letters that work together to produce a vowel sound. The vowel sound may be long, short, or a diphthong (gliding monosyllabic speech sound).

Example: Decode: ex|plain (Cl | VT; v c | c v) Encode: e x p l a i n

re|gain (O | VT; v | c v)

hang|nail

main|tain (VT | VT; v c | c v)

plain|tiff (VT | Cl; v c | c v)

stain|less (VT | Cl; v c | c v)

Syllable Type 4: Vowel Team (VT) ai

Sentences

Have students practice reading sentences for automaticity. These can also be used for dictation.

1. Who will remain on stage when the contest has ended?
2. The plaintiff will refrain from comment.
3. It is not safe to tailgate when you drive.
4. The actress will maintain her big role in the film.
5. Did the goblin take the red paintbrush and wash it?
6. Gail will fuss if the mailman is late.
7. The pole for the mailbox is bent and broken.
8. The bailiff had to lead the witness to the stand.
9. Gail bit the hangnail.
10. The frail man cannot maintain a smile.
11. What steps does the plan entail?
12. Let me explain why I lost the document.
13. Will the plaintiff win the case?

Syllable Type 4: Vowel Team (VT) ay

A Vowel Team (VT) is two, three, or four letters that work together to produce a vowel sound. The vowel sound may be long, short, or a diphthong (gliding monosyllabic speech sound).

Example: Decode: Fri|day (O | VT; v|c v) Encode: Friday

sub|way	Cl | VT	v c | c v
es|say	Cl | VT	v c | c v
Sun|day	Cl | VT	v c | c v
dis|may	Cl | VT	v c | c v
Bom|bay	Cl | VT	v c | c v
dis|play	Cl | VT	v c | c v
cray|fish	VT | Cl	v | c v
rail|way	VT | VT	v c | c v
may|be	VT | O	v | c v
play|time	VT | ME	v | c v
may|hem	VT | Cl	v | c v
play|mate	VT | ME	v | c v
re|lay	O | VT	v|c v
pay|ment	VT | Cl	v | c v
Fri|day	O | VT	v|c v
de|lay	O | VT	v|c v

Syllable Type 4: Vowel Team (VT) ay

A Vowel Team (VT) is two, three, or four letters that work together to produce a vowel sound. The vowel sound may be long, short, or a diphthong (gliding monosyllabic speech sound).

Example: Decode: Fri|day (O | VT; v|c v) Encode: F r i d a y

de|cay (O | VT; v|c v)

free|way (VT | VT; v|c v)

may|pole (VT | ME; v|c v)

hay|seed (VT | VT; v|c v)

hay|ride (VT | ME; v|c v)

dis|may (Cl | VT; v c|c v)

ash|tray (Cl | VT; v c|c v)

main|stay (VT | VT; v c|c v)

Syllable Type 4: Vowel Team (VT) ay

Sentences

Have students practice reading sentences for automaticity. These can also be used for dictation.

1. Did you submit the payment for the bill?
2. Jay can run fast and may help the team win the relay.
3. When traffic is bad, I hate to drive on the freeway.
4. On Friday, Jay will display his talent when he plays the trombone in public.
5. Maybe the candy will not melt in the hot sun.
6. Quentin has plans to go on a solo trip to Bombay next week.
7. The playmates had a blast on the hayride!
8. Your teeth will decay if you do not brush and floss.
9. The student must fix the mistakes on his essay by Friday, or he will fail the class.
10. The crash on the freeway will lead to a long delay.
11. Crayfish inhabit the fresh stream.
12. It will be mayhem on the freeway, so it is best to take the subway.
13. The ashtray stunk, so Kay had to clean it with bleach.
14. The hayseed made me sneeze and itch.
15. Will the insects eat the mainstay crop?

Syllable Type 4: Vowel Team (VT) oa

A Vowel Team (VT) is two, three, or four letters that work together to produce a vowel sound. The vowel sound may be long, short, or a diphthong (gliding monosyllabic speech sound).

Example: Decode: co|coa (O | VT; v|c v) Encode: c o c o a

be|moan (O | VT; v|c v)	soap|box (VT | Cl; v c|c v)	coat|tail (VT | VT; v c|c v)
coast|line (VT | ME; v c|c v)	steam|boat (VT | VT; v c|c v)	rail|road (VT | VT; v c|c v)
in|road (Cl | VT; v c|c v)	toad|stone (VT | ME; v c|c v)	sail|boat (VT | VT; v c|c v)
en|croach (Cl | VT; v c|c v)	un|load (Cl | VT; v c|c v)	
oat|meal (VT | VT; v c|c v)	co|coa (O | VT; v|c v)	
pea|coat (VT | VT; v|c v)	cross|road (Cl | VT; v c|c v)	
re|load (O | VT; v|c v)	en|croach|ment (Cl | VT | Cl; v c|c v c|c v)	
re|proach (O | VT)	tail|coat (VT | VT; v c|c v)	

Syllable Type 4: Vowel Team (VT) oa

Sentences

Have students practice reading sentences for automaticity. These can also be used for dictation.

1. Joan likes to drive by the Atlantic coastline.
2. The coach gave the team hot cocoa with cream.
3. The toad croaked while it was on the steamboat.
4. Help the coach reload the van.
5. Do not encroach upon the foal while it roams.
6. Joan will moan and groan if her oatmeal is steamy.
7. The steamboat will chug a load of coal.
8. A roach ran around the dish of oatmeal.
9. Will the toadstone help the men in combat?
10. Mom must reproach Dustin when he has a tantrum.
11. Maxwell will not bemoan a loss at tennis.
12. Jan will moan if you make her put on a peacoat.
13. Joan will help Jane unload the boat.
14. Go to the left when you reach the crossroad.
15. At the end of playtime, the students like to drink cocoa.

Syllable Type 4: Vowel Team (VT) oe

A Vowel Team (VT) is two, three, or four letters that work together to produce a vowel sound. The vowel sound may be long, short, or a diphthong (gliding monosyllabic speech sound).

Example: Decode: tip|toe (Cl | VT; v c | c v) Encode: t i p t o e

roe|buck (VT | Cl; v | c v)

Ros|coe (Cl | VT; v c | c v)

tip|toe (Cl | VT; v c | c v)

toe|nail (VT | VT; v | c v)

o|boe (O | VT; v | c v)

pe|koe (O | VT; v | c v)

al|oe (Cl | VT; v c | v)

woe|ful (VT | Cl; v | c v)

toe|cap (VT | Cl; v | c v)

Have students practice reading sentences for automaticity. These can also be used for dictation.

1. Joe can play the oboe, and Jay can play the trombone.
2. Joan likes to paint her toenails pink.
3. Sammy was woeful when he broke the plastic robot.
4. The coach must stand on tiptoe to reach the equipment.
5. Pekoe is a fine tea.

Decoding Words with Suffix -ing

Have students practice circling the suffix -ing and then decode the rest of the word if needed.

Example: Decode: d a s h | (i n g)   Encode: d a s h + (i n g)

itch | (ing)	wish | (ing)	bend | (ing)
flash | (ing)	say | (ing)	camp | (ing)
dash | (ing)	buzz | (ing)	un | pack | (ing) (Cl Cl; v c | c v)
play | (ing)	fin | ish | (ing) (Cl Cl; v c | v)	dump | (ing)
van | ish | (ing) (Cl Cl; v c | v)	aim | (ing)	hunt | (ing)
fry | (ing)	box | (ing)	soak | (ing)
bail | (ing)	dry | (ing)	yell | (ing)
boat | (ing)	cling | (ing)	de | lay | (ing) (O VT; v | c v)

Decoding Words with Suffix -ing

Have students practice circling the suffix -ing and then decode the rest of the word if needed.

Example: Decode: d a s h | i n g   Encode: d a s h + i n g

O | Cl e | l e c t | ing v | c v	Cl | VT o | p e n | ing v | c v	Cl | Cl i m | p a c t | ing v c | c v
O | VT e | m a i l | ing v | c v	O | Cl r e | q u e s t | ing v | c v	Cl | Cl i n | v e s t | ing v c | c v
Cl | Cl u n | h i t c h | ing v c | c v	O | Cl d e | p e n d | ing v | c v	
Cl | VT u n | l e a s h | ing v c | c v	O | VT d e | t a i l | ing v | c v	

Decoding Words with Suffix -ing

Sentences

Have students practice reading sentences for automaticity. These can also be used for dictation.

1. Cindy was unpacking the boxes when she saw a slimy toad.
2. Is the hotel opening this weekend?
3. Mom was yelling when the snake slid down the path.
4. The vanishing act seemed like magic to the students.
5. We are investing in stocks and land.
6. The team is camping on the hillside with tents and sleeping bags.
7. The dog is finishing his meal quickly when he is hungry.
8. Why is the robot requesting a treat?
9. Steve is telling a funny joke, and Shantel is going to miss it.
10. Are you electing to go fishing in the pond or the big lake?
11. The foxes were sprinting down the road to catch up with the dogs.
12. That truck was dumping rocks in the deep, muddy ditch.
13. When Stan was drying the dishes, he made a mistake and broke a plate.

Decoding Words with Suffix -ing

Sentences

Have students practice reading sentences for automaticity. These can also be used for dictation.

14. The rain is delaying the plane from flying on time.
15. Who is emailing the details for the contest?
16. I yelled when the bee was buzzing by my neck.
17. The hippo was not soaking in the bathtub the last time we checked on him.
18. The wind is impacting the way the kite is flying.
19. Brandy and Tim are playing with the cute puppy.
20. My skin was itching from being in the thick, prickly bushes.

Three-Consonant Blends and Blends with Digraphs

Consonant blends are made up of two to three graphemes. Each phoneme represented by the graphemes is heard in a blend. Consonant blends occur at the beginning or end of syllables.

Example: Decode: s p l e n | d i d (Cl | Cl; v c | c v) Encode: s p l e n d i d

an|thrax (Cl | Cl)	off|screen (Cl | VT)	screen|play (VT | VT)
splen|did (Cl | Cl)	en|shrine (Cl | ME)	off|spring (Cl)
in|struct (Cl | Cl)	stream|line (VT | ME)	thrif|ty (Cl | O)
ab|stract (Cl | Cl)	sub|scribe (Cl | ME)	
ham|string (Cl)	sun|screen (Cl | VT)	
tran|scribe (Cl | ME)	tran|script (Cl | Cl)	
seam|stress (VT | Cl)	in|scribe (Cl | ME)	
main|stream (VT | VT)		

Please note:
After the first two vowels are underlined and labeled, look for consonants. If there are more than two, look for known digraphs or blends to be labeled as one consonant unit. Beginning R Blends and L Blends are the most common.

Three-Consonant Blends and Blends with Digraphs

Sentences

Have students practice reading sentences for automaticity. These can also be used for dictation.

1. Edwin will transcribe the note when Shantel gives it to him.
2. Do not entrap the splendid frog.
3. Who will instruct the students?
4. We could not see the actress when she was offscreen.
5. Sunscreen will help protect you from the rays of the sun.
6. The seamstress made a velvet dress for the princess.
7. Sammy can save by trying to be thrifty.
8. Where is the abstract painting on display?
9. Fran and I will read the transcript from the program.

Schwa

Schwa is the most common vowel sound in the English language. It can be spelled with any of the 5 vowels. It typically sounds like /ŭ/ or /ĭ/. Schwa is never in a stressed syllable.

Example: Decode: gal|lon (Cl | Cl; v c|c v) Encode: g a l l o n

ba|con (O | Cl; v|c v)	ac|quaint (Cl | VT; v c| c v)	dis|con|nect (Cl | Cl | C; v c|c v c|c v)
con|fess (Cl | Cl; v c|c v)	crim|son (Cl | Cl; v c|c v)	in|tel|lect (Cl | Cl | Cl; v c|c v c|c v)
fos|sil (Cl | Cl; v c|c v)	prob|lem (Cl | Cl; v c|c v)	in|di|rect (Cl | O | Cl; v c|c v|c v)
gal|lon (Cl | Cl; v c|c v)	em|blem (Cl | Cl; v c| c v)	col|lect (Cl | Cl; v c|c v)
ma|son (O | Cl; v|c v)	con|ceal (Cl | VT; v c|c v)	com|mand (Cl | Cl; v c|c v)
to|tem (O | Cl; v|c v)	ad|just (Cl | Cl; v c|c v)	nos|tril (Cl | Cl; v c| c v)
i|tem (O | Cl; v|c v)	con|sist (Cl | Cl; v c|c v)	ap|pen|dix (Cl | Cl | Cl; v c|c v c|c v)
oc|to|pus (Cl | O | Cl; v c|c v|c v)	con|fide (Cl | ME; v c|c v)	hip|po|pot|a|mus (Cl | O | Cl | O | Cl; v c|c v|c v c|v|c v)

Schwa

Schwa is the most common vowel sound in the English language. It can be spelled with any of the 5 vowels. It typically sounds like /ŭ/ or /ĭ/. Schwa is never in a stressed syllable.

Example: Decode: g a l | l o n (Cl | Cl; v c | c v) Encode: g a l l o n

daf | fo | dil (Cl | O | Cl; v c | c v | c v)	an | te | lope (Cl | O | ME; v c | c v | c v)	croc | o | dile (Cl | O | ME; v c | v | c v)
dip | lo | mat (Cl | O | Cl; v c | c v | c v)	con | fis | cate (Cl | Cl | ME; v c | c v c | c v)	con | tain (Cl | VT; v c | c v)
ab | do | men (Cl | O | Cl; v c | c v | c v)	ob | so | lete (Cl | O | ME; v c | c v | c v)	com | plain (Cl | VT; v c | c v)
a | dopt (O | Cl; v | c v)	lam | i | nate (Cl | O | ME; v c | v | c v)	ob | tain (Cl | VT; v c | c v)
com | bine (Cl | ME; v c | c v)	max | i | mum (Cl | O | Cl; v c | v | c v)	ac | claim (Cl | VT; v c | c v)
com | plete (Cl | ME; v c | c v)	lem | o | nade (Cl | O | ME; v c | v | c v)	
com | mit | tee (Cl | Cl | VT; v c | c v c | c v)	ju | bi | lee (O | O | VT; v | c v | c v)	

Schwa

Sentences

Have students practice reading sentences for automaticity. These can also be used for dictation.

1. Jim cannot commit to the job until he is finished with the project.
2. The problems on the math test are complex.
3. The class constructed a boat out of sticks.
4. The mastiff dug up a hundred fossils.
5. My glasses need an adjustment to fit.
6. Did Alfred land at the bottom of the steep hill when he fell?
7. Mom had to confiscate Fido's stash of bones.
8. The sub gave the class a math page to complete yesterday.
9. A maximum of seven people can fit in the dumptruck.
10. Kevin is confident that he can win the contest.
11. If you approach the toad, it will croak.
12. The actress will win acclaim for her big role in the film.
13. You should not complain when you open the gift.
14. The committee will vote on the rule.
15. I could smell the bacon when I walked to the stove.

Schwa

Sentences

Have students practice reading sentences for automaticity. These can also be used for dictation.

16. The hippopotamus will not fit in the basket.
17. I had pink lemonade and muffins for lunch today.
18. The gallon of white milk fell off the shelf and made a mess.
19. Where is the daffodil I left on the side of the road?
20. The queen was so impressed that she gave the seamstress a compliment.

Syllable Type 5: Bossy R (BR) er

(also called r-controlled)

The "r" controls the vowel and produces an entirely new sound.

Example: Decode: per|tain (BR | VT; v | c v) Encode: p e r t a i n

ad|vert (CI | BR; v c | c v)	ther|mo|me|ter (BR | CI | O | BR; v | c v c | v | c v)
af|ter|math (CI | BR | CI; v c | c v | c v)	cul|vert (CI | BR; v c | c v)
Al|ex|an|der (CI | CI | CI | BR; v c | v c | v c | c v)	ot|ter (CI | BR; v c | c v)
ant|ler (CI | BR; v c | c v)	af|ter|time (CI | BR | ME; v c | c v | c v)
blis|ter (CI | BR; v c | c v)	ad|min|is|ter (CI | CI | CI | BR; v c | c v c | v c | c v)
lus|ter (CI | BR; v c | c v)	ad|verb (CI | BR; v c | c v)
pros|per (CI | BR; v c | c v)	her|mit (BR | CI; v | c v)
raf|ter (CI | BR; v c | c v)	lit|ter (CI | BR; v c | c v)

Syllable Type 5: Bossy R (BR) er

(also called r-controlled)

The "r" controls the vowel and produces an entirely new sound.

Example: Decode: per|tain (BR | VT; v | c v) Encode: pertain

*Be careful when dividing syllables with Bossy R. If there is a known blend, it may stay together. In addition, compound words are split between each smaller word.

can|is|ter (Cl | Cl | BR; v c | v c | c v)

bit|ter|sweet* (Cl | BR | VT; v c | c v | c v)

block|bus|ter (Cl | Cl | BR; v c | c v c | c v)

blun|der (Cl | BR; v c | c v)

but|ter|nut (Cl | BR | Cl; v c | c v | c v)

cack|ler (Cl | BR; v c | c v)

blus|ter (Cl | BR; v c | c v)

cas|ter (Cl | BR; v c | c v)

ca|ter (O | BR; v | c v)

chand|ler (Cl | BR; v c | c v)

ver|dict (BR | Cl; v | c v)

ham|ster (Cl | BR; v c | c v)

mut|ter (Cl | BR; v c | c v)

lan|tern (Cl | BR; v c | c v)

per|plex* (BR | Cl; v | c v)

ver|min (BR | Cl; v | c v)

Syllable Type 5: Bossy R (BR) er

(also called r-controlled)

The "r" controls the vowel and produces an entirely new sound.

Example: Decode: per|tain (BR | VT; v | c v) Encode: pertain

*Be careful when dividing syllables with Bossy R. If there is a known blend, it may stay together. In addition, compound words are split between each smaller word.

bea|ver (VT | BR; v | c v)	cler|gy (BR | O; v | c v)
ex|pert (CI | BR; v c | c v)	en|ter|tain (CI | BR | VT; v c | v c | c v)
per|sist (BR | CI; v | c v)	ter|mi|nate (BR | O | ME; v | c v | c v)
ver|bose (BR | ME; v | c v)	ex|ter|mi|nate (CI | BR | O | ME; v c | c v | c v | c v)
in|fer|no (CI | BR | O; v c | c v | c v)	chat|ter|box (CI | BR | CI; v c | c v | c v)
pep|per|mint (CI | BR | CI; v c | c v | c v)	lob|ster (CI | BR; v c | c v)
im|pos|ter (CI | CI | BR; v c | c v c | c v)	ber|serk (BR | BR; v | c v)
scat|ter|brain* (CI | BR | VT; v c | c v | c v)	clut|ter (CI | BR; v c | c v)

Syllable Type 5: Bossy R (BR) er

(also called r-controlled)

The "r" controls the vowel and produces an entirely new sound.

Example: Decode: per|tain (BR | VT; v | c v) Encode: p e r t a i n

twit|ter (Cl | BR; v c | c v)	pam|per (Cl | BR; v c | c v)
stut|ter (Cl | BR; v c | c v)	wes|tern (Cl | BR; v c | c v)
clea|ner (VT | BR; v | c v) *or* clean|er (VT | BR)	ves|per (Cl | BR; v c | c v)
per|fume (BR | ME; v | c v)	hin|der (Cl | BR; v c | c v)
per|fect (BR | Cl; v | c v)	scam|per (Cl | BR; v c | c v)
al|ler|gy (Cl | BR | O; v c | c v | c v)	ter|mite (BR | ME; v | c v)
plun|der (Cl | BR; v c | c v)	ros|ter (Cl | BR; v c | c v)
clo|ver|leaf (O | BR | VT; v | c v | c v)	ver|tex (BR | Cl; v | c v)

Syllable Type 5: Bossy R (BR) er

(also called r-controlled)

The "r" controls the vowel and produces an entirely new sound.

Example: Decode: per|tain (BR | VT; v | c v) Encode: p e r t a i n

*Be careful when dividing syllables with Bossy R. If there is a known blend, it may stay together. In addition, compound words are split between each smaller word.

per|vade (BR | ME; v | c v)

ut|ter (Cl | BR; v c | c v)

Am|ster|dam (Cl | BR | Cl; v c | c v | c v)

cin|der (Cl | BR; v c | c v)

gin|ger (Cl | BR; v c | c v)

ger|mane (BR | ME; v | c v)

mer|cy (BR | O; v | c v)

cy|ber|space* (O | BR | ME; v | c v | c v)

in|ter|sect (Cl | BR | Cl; v c | c v | c v)

sus|pen|der (Cl | Cl | BR; v c | c v c | c v)

in|ter|rupt (Cl | BR | Cl; v c | c v | c v)

Syllable Type 5: Bossy R (BR) er

Sentences

Have students practice reading sentences for automaticity. These can also be used for dictation.

*Be careful when dividing syllables with Bossy R. If there is a known blend, it may stay together. In addition, compound words are split between each smaller word.

1. The perfume has a strong smell.
2. The silver ring lost its luster, so the preacher had to polish it.
3. Speak up! Do not mutter when you read.
4. Will the complex math problem perplex* the student?
5. The hamster likes to run on the wheel.
6. Will the beaver cross the dam?
7. Coach Ernest will provide the roster next week.
8. The butler will never complain to the maid.
9. The teacher is a math expert.
10. The athlete will persist in spite of pain and will cross the finish line.
11. Run fast to escape the inferno!
12. If you interrupt Gertrude* when she is speaking, she will scream.
13. Interpret the map to see if the roads intersect.
14. Drink peppermint tea when you do not feel well.
15. Herbert is a scatterbrain* and cannot remember if he ate dinner.

Syllable Type 5: Bossy R (BR) er

Sentences

Have students practice reading sentences for automaticity. These can also be used for dictation.

16. Ernest will entertain us by playing the oboe.
17. Will the boss terminate the contract?
18. The teacher will administer the exam.
19. Put the thermometer in the container so that it will not shatter if you drop it.
20. Alexander will not pester the butler.
21. Herbert must exterminate the termites.

Syllable Type 5: Bossy R (BR) ir

(also called r-controlled)

The "r" controls the vowel and produces an entirely new sound.

Example: Decode: vir|gule (BR | ME; v|c v) Encode: v i r g u l e***

bird|bath (BR | CI; v c|c v)	jay|bird (VT | BR; v|c v)
bird|seed (BR | VT; v c|c v)	mirth|less (BR | CI; v c|c v)
birth|stone (BR | ME; v c|c v)	red|shirt (CI | BR; v c|c v)
con|firm (CI | BR; v c|c v)	sea|bird (VT | BR; v|c v)
fir|kin (BR | CI; v|c v)	squirt|ed (/id/)
flirt|ed (/id/)	stir|rup (BR | CI; v|c v)
hum|ming|bird (CI | | BR; v c|c v|c v)	thir|teen (BR | VT; v|c v)
in|firm (CI | BR; v c|c v)	thun|der|bird (CI | BR | BR; v c|c v|c v)

Syllable Type 5: Bossy R (BR) ir

(also called r-controlled)

The "r" controls the vowel and produces an entirely new sound.

Example: Decode: vir|gule (BR | ME; v|c v) Encode: virgule***

twir|ling (BR; v|c v) *or* twirl|ing (BR)	birth|day (BR | VT; v c | c v)
un|der|shirt (Cl | BR | BR; v c | c v | c v)	skir|mish (BR | Cl; v | c v)
vir|gate (BR | ME; v | c v)	Bir|ming|ham (BR | | Cl; v | c v | c v)
vir|gule (BR | ME; v | c v)	
zir|con (BR | Cl; v | c v)	
e|lix|ir (O | Cl | BR; v | c v c | v)	
birth|date (BR | ME; v c | c v)	
Vir|go (BR | O; v | c v)	

Syllable Type 5: Bossy R (BR) ir

Sentences

Have students practice reading sentences for automaticity. These can also be used for dictation.

1. The infirm man was too weak to stand up.
2. Alexander will be thirteen on his next birthday.
3. Does Irving consider Friday the thirteenth a day to be afraid?
4. Send an email to Irwin to confirm the meeting.
5. A skirmish between the players made the coaches end the game.
6. Adding a birthstone to the silver ring will make it a perfect gift.
7. The jay likes to swim in the birdbath.
8. Irwin's birthdate is the day after mine.
9. Will the cat jump up and consume the birdseed?
10. The coach had to redshirt the athlete and develop his skills.
11. The hummingbird will relax in the birdbath.
12. Irwin will confirm the time of the meeting so that he is not late.
13. Irving did not stop in Birmingham because he still had to drive a long way.
14. Do you think the thunderbird will alert us of thunder?

Syllable Type 5: Bossy R (BR) ur

(also called r - controlled)

The "r" controls the vowel and produces an entirely new sound.

Example: Decode: t u r | n i p (BR | Cl; v | c v)   Encode: t u r n i p

*Be careful when dividing syllables with Bossy R. If there is a known blend, it may stay together.

Cl | BR d i s | t u r b v c | c v	BR | O | Cl b u r | g o | n e t v | c v | c v
BR | ME s u r | v i v e v | c v	BR | ME c u r b | s i d e v c | c v
BR | Cl t u r | b a n v | c v	O | BR | BR o | v e r | t u r n v | c v | c v
BR | BR b l u r | t e r v | c v	BR | Cl b u r | l a p v | c v
BR | Cl s u r | p l u s * v | c v	BR | BR c u r | l e r v | c v
Cl | BR b u l | g u r v c | c v	BR | Cl b u r | n e t v | c v
BR | BR m u r | m u r v | c v	BR | O b u r | r o v | c v
BR | Cl b u r | d e n v | c v	Cl | BR | BR h a m | b u r | g e r v c | c v | c v

Syllable Type 5: Bossy R (BR) ur

(also called r - controlled)

The "r" controls the vowel and produces an entirely new sound.

Example: Decode: turnip (BR | Cl) Encode: turnip

furnisher (BR | Cl | BR)	exurb (Cl | BR)
concur (Cl | BR)	curtail (BR | VT)
hurdler (BR | BR)	femur (O | BR)
incur (Cl | BR)	curriculum (BR | Cl | O | Cl)
concurrent (Cl | BR | Cl)	furbish (BR | Cl)
perturb (BR | BR)	further (BR | BR)
frankfurter (| BR | BR)	urgent (BR | Cl)

Syllable Type 5: Bossy R (BR) ur

(also called r - controlled)

The "r" controls the vowel and produces an entirely new sound.

Example: Decode: t u r | n i p (BR | Cl; v | c v)   Encode: t u r n i p

*Be careful when dividing syllables with Bossy R. If there is a known blend, it may stay together.

BR | Cl
c u r | r e n t
v | c v

BR | ME
t u r n | s t i l e
v c | c v

BR | Cl | ME
t u r | p e n | t i n e
v | c v c | c v

BR | Cl | O
u r | g e n | c y
v | c v c | c v

Cl | BR
s u b | u r b
v c | v

BR | Cl | BR
s u r | r e n | d e r
v | c v c | c v

BR | O | ME
h u r | r i | c a n e
v | c v | c v

Syllable Type 5: Bossy R (BR) ur

Sentences

Have students practice reading sentences for automaticity. These can also be used for dictation.

*Be careful when dividing syllables with Bossy R. If there is a known blend, it may stay together.

1. Gertrude* will help furnish the den with eclectic objects.
2. Fill the burlap bag with birdseed to feed to the hummingbirds.
3. Westminster is a suburb of Denver.
4. Speak up! If you murmur, you will not win the debate.
5. If you perturb Herbert the butler, he may quit.
6. Use the surplus* fabric from the dress to make a skirt.
7. Never jump over the turnstile to the subway!
8. Use turpentine to get a paint stain off a rug.
9. The combat will go on until one side agrees to surrender.
10. I will order a thick hamburger with crisp bacon, tomato, and peanut butter.
11. Frank likes to grill frankfurters and slather them in fresh tomatoes.
12. You must seek shelter to protect your children from the hurricane.

Syllable Pattern 4: (V/V)

The last syllable pattern taught is vowel/vowel.

Example: Decode: vi|o|lin (O | O | CI; v v c v)   Encode: v i o l i n

po|et (O | CI; v v)	vid|e|o (CI | O | O; v c v v)	di|ag|nose (O | CI | ME; v v c c v)
po|em (O | CI; v v)	di|a|lect (O | O | CI; v v c v)	ro|de|o (O | O | O; v c v v)
cre|ate (O | ME; v v)	o|a|sis (O | O | CI; v v c v)	
cam|e|o (CI | O | O; v c v v)	vi|o|lent (O | O | CI; v v c v)	

Have students practice reading sentences for automaticity. These can also be used for dictation.

1. The poet will create a poem.
2. The actress had a cameo in the skit.
3. The Midwest dialect is different than the west coast.
4. I need to go to an oasis to relax.
5. The rodeo was fun.

Syllable Type 4: Vowel Team (VT) oi (diphthong)

This vowel team is a diphthong. Di means two, and phthong means sound. A diphthong starts in one manner of articulation and glides into another. A syllable with a diphthong will be labeled as VT (Vowel Team).

"Oi" (/oi/) is found at the beginning and in the middle of words and syllables (e.g., oil, boil).

Example: Decode: goi|ter (VT | BR; v | c v) Encode: g o i t e r

ex|ploit (Cl | VT; v c | c v)	sir|loin (BR | VT; v | c v)
as|ter|oid (Cl | BR | VT; v c | c v | v)	tur|moil (BR | VT; v | c v)
goi|ter (VT | BR; v | c v)	oint|ment (VT | Cl; v c | c v)
oil|skin (VT | Cl; v c | c v)	tab|loid (Cl | VT; v c | c v)
oil|cloth (VT | Cl; v c | c v)	ten|der|loin (Cl | BR | VT; v c | c v | c v)
poi|son (VT | Cl; v | c v)	de|void (O | VT; v | c v)
tin|foil (Cl | VT; v c | c v)	trap|e|zoid (Cl | O | VT; v c | v | c v)

Syllable Type 4: Vowel Team (VT) oi (diphthong)

This vowel team is a diphthong. Di means two, and phthong means sound. A diphthong starts in one manner of articulation and glides into another. A syllable with a diphthong will be labeled as VT (Vowel Team).

"Oi" (/oi/) is found at the beginning and in the middle of words and syllab es (e.g., oil, boil).

Example: Decode: goi | ter (VT | BR; v | c v) Encode: g oi t e r

loi | ter (VT | BR; v | c v)

re | coil (O | VT; v | c v)

del | toid (Cl | VT; v c | c v)

stand | point (Cl | VT; v c | c v)

clois | ter (VT | BR; v c | c v)

em | broi | der (Cl | VT | BR; v c | c v | c v)

Syllable Type 4: Vowel Team (VT) oi (diphthong)

Sentences

Have students practice reading sentences for automaticity. These can also be used for dictation.

1. Mom will not even skim a tabloid while she waits in line to pay.
2. Albert put tinfoil around the meat to keep it hot until we could eat.
3. The ointment will help stop Fido's skin problem.
4. Jennifer is still in a state of turmoil.
5. Fresh sirloin makes the best hamburgers.
6. Fernando is content to cloister himself at home.
7. I will recoil if I see a rat, a snake, or a cockroach.
8. The acrobat has strong deltoids, which help her master handstands.
9. The fisherman stayed dry in his oilskin coat.
10. The teacher helped the math students make a trapezoid.
11. The poison in the snake's bite can make you sick.
12. The seamstress will embroider a silver coin on the denim pants.
13. Felix will broil the tenderloin for dinner.
14. We hope to see an asteroid in the sky.

Syllable Type 4: Vowel Team (VT) oy (diphthong)

This vowel team is a diphthong. Di means two, and phthong means sound. A diphthong starts in one manner of articulation and glides into another. A syllable with a diphthong will be labeled as VT (Vowel Team).

"Oy" (/oi/) is found at the end of words and syllables (e.g., boy).

Example: Decode: em|ploy (Cl | VT; v c | c v) Encode: e m p l o y

en|joy (Cl | VT; v c | c v)	de|coy (O | VT; v | c v)
tom|boy (Cl | VT; v c | c v)	em|ploy|ment (Cl | VT | Cl; v c | c v | c v)
em|ploy (Cl | VT; v c | c v)	roy|al (VT | Cl; v | v)
boy|cott (VT | Cl; v | c v)	foy|er (VT | BR; v | v)
oy|ster* (VT | BR; v c v)	soy|bean (VT | VT; v | c v)
dis|loy|al (Cl | VT | Cl; v c | c v | v)	an|noy (Cl | VT; v c | c v)
de|stroy (O | VT; v | c v)	con|voy (Cl | VT; v c | c v)

* In this word, the "st" blend stays together.

Syllable Type 4: Vowel Team (VT) oy (diphthong)

This vowel team is a diphthong. Di means two, and phthong means sound. A diphthong starts in one manner of articulation and glides into another. A syllable with a diphthong will be labeled as VT (Vowel Team).

"Oy" (/oi/) is found at the end of words and syllables (e.g., boy).

Example: Decode: e m | p l o y (Cl | VT; v c | c v) Encode: e m p l o y

d e | p l o y (O | VT; v | c v)

e m | p l o y | e e (Cl | VT | VT; v c | c v | v)

a l | l o y (Cl | VT; v c | c v)

d i s | l o y | a l (Cl | VT | Cl; v c | c v | v)

j o y | f u l (VT | Cl; v | c v)

t o y | s h o p (VT | Cl; v | c v)

b e l l | b o y (Cl | VT; v c | c v)

f l a m | b o y | a n t (Cl | VT | Cl; v c | c v | v)

Syllable Type 4: Vowel Team (VT) oy (diphthong)

Sentences

Have students practice reading sentences for automaticity. These can also be used for dictation.

1. Roy the cowboy trains for the rodeo in Texas.
2. Dustin's temper tantrums are annoying to his sisters.
3. For the winter holidays, the staff will decorate the foyer of the hotel in rich velvet.
4. Never eat an oyster unless it is fresh.
5. The activists will boycott the fur shop.
6. The hunter will use a decoy to attract birds.
7. A convoy of Jeeps will take the men to the combat zone.
8. The employee enjoys his job at the toy shop.
9. Roy does not enjoy shucking oysters.
10. Combine metallic elements to create an alloy.
11. The subject was disloyal to the royal king.
12. Nate will seek employment after he is finished with the summer project.
13. Joy got a flamboyant dress for her date with the royal king.

Syllable Type 4: Vowel Team (VT) ou (diphthong)

This vowel team is a diphthong. Di means two, and phthong means sound. A diphthong starts in one manner of articulation and glides into another. A syllable with a diphthong will be labeled as VT (Vowel Team).

"Ou" /ou/ is found at the beginning and in the middle of words and syllables (e.g., out, snout).

Example: Decode: VT | ME
o u t | l i n e
v c | c v

Encode: o u t l i n e***

Cl | VT
b a d | m o u t h
v c | c v

VT | VT
b a i l | o u t
v c | v

BR | VT
b u r n | o u t
v c | v

Cl | VT
c h e c k | o u t
v c | v

O | VT
c o | f o u n d
v | c v

Cl | VT
c o m | p o u n d
v c | c v

VT | BR | VT
c o u n | t e r | p o i n t
v c | c v | c v

O | VT
d e | v o u t
v | c v

Cl | VT
d i s | c o u n t
v c | c v

Cl | VT
e x | p o u n d
v c | c v

Cl | VT
i m | p o u n d
v c | c v

VT | Cl
c o u n | t e s s
v c | c v

VT | BR
f o u n | d e r
v c | c v

VT | BR
f l o u n | d e r
v c | c v

Syllable Type 4: Vowel Team (VT) ou (diphthong)

This vowel team is a diphthong. Di means two, and phthong means sound. A diphthong starts in one manner of articulation and glides into another. A syllable with a diphthong will be labeled as VT (Vowel Team).

"Ou" /ou/ is found at the beginning and in the middle of words and syllables (e.g., out, snout).

Example: Decode: out|line (VT | ME; v c|c v) Encode: outline***

*Be careful when dividing syllables with Bossy R. If there is a known blenc, it may stay together. In addition, compound words are split between each smaller word.

VT | BR | Cl | VT
coun|ter|com|plaint
v c|c v|c v c|c v

VT | ME
out|line
v c|c v

VT | Cl
roun|dup
v c|c v

VT | O | VT
roun|da|bout
v c|c v|c v

O | VT
pro|noun
v|c v

Cl | BR | VT
thun|der|cloud*
v c|c v|c v

VT | Cl | Cl
out|lan|dish
v c|c v c|c v

BR | VT
sur|round
v|c v

VT | Cl
ground|hog
v c|c v

Cl | VT
as|tound
v c|c v

O | VT
pro|found
v|c v

VT | Cl
out|stan|ding
v c|c v c|c v

or

VT | Cl
out|stand|ing
v c|c v

Syllable Type 4: Vowel Team (VT) ou (diphthong)

Sentences

Have students practice reading sentences for automaticity. These can also be used for dictation.

1. Run to the fish shop and get a pound of flounder.
2. The job of a pronoun is to fill in for a noun.
3. When you need to create an essay, make an outline first.
4. Maxwell is a devout tennis fan.
5. The dentist will discount her rate if you cannot pay the fee.
6. The profound statements prompted the students to think deeply.
7. The sweet sound of the band will astound you.
8. Groundhog is a compound noun.
9. Can a groundhog predict the end of winter?
10. The grouch had an outstanding essay about the founder of the town.
11. Will the actress don an outlandish dress?
12. The scout who spoke in a roundabout manner lost the debate.
13. Coach Kevin did not let the team play outside until the thundercloud went away.

Syllable Type 4: Vowel Team (VT) ow (diphthong)

This vowel team is a diphthong. Di means two, and phthong means sound. A diphthong starts in one manner of articulation and glides into another. A syllable with a diphthong will be labeled as VT (Vowel Team).

"Ow" /ou/ is found at the end of words and syllables (e.g., now, pow/er, tow/el) and before "l" or "n" (e.g., howl, down).

Example: Decode: VT | BR
p o w | e r
v | v

Encode: p o w e r

Cl | VT | BR
b e l l | f l o w | e r
v c | c v | v

VT | VT
c o w | b o y
v | c v

VT | BR
c o w | e r
v | v

VT | ME
c o w | h i d e
v | c v

VT | BR
p o w | e r
v | v

VT | Cl
t o w | e l
v | v

VT | ME
d o w n | g r a d e
v c | c v

VT | BR
f l o w | e r
v | v

VT | BR
s h o w | e r
v | v

Cl | VT | BR
s a f | f l o w | e r
v c | c v | v

VT | BR
p o w | d e r
v | c v

VT | BR
c h o w | d e r
v | c v

VT | VT
d o w n | l o a d
v c | c v

Syllable Type 4: Vowel Team (VT) ow (diphthong)

This vowel team is a diphthong. Di means two, and phthong means sound. A diphthong starts in one manner of articulation and glides into another. A syllable with a diphthong will be labeled as VT (Vowel Team).

"Ow" /ou/ is found at the end of words and syllables (e.g., now, pow/er, tow/el) and before "l" or "n" (e.g., howl, down).

Example: Decode: VT | BR — p o w | e r — v | v Encode: p o w e r

Syllable types	Word	Vowel/consonant marks
VT | ME	d o w n | s i z e	v c | c v
VT | VT	d o w n | t o w n	v c | c v
Cl | VT	e n | d o w	v c | c v
VT | Cl | BR	h o w | e v | e r	v | v c | v
VT | Cl	v o w | e l	v | v
Cl | VT | BR	m a n | p o w | e r	v c | c v | v
O | VT	m e | o w	v | v

Syllable types	Word	Vowel/consonant marks
O | BR | VT | BR	o | v e r | p o w | e r	v | c v | c v | v
Cl | VT	s u n | d o w n	v c | c v
VT | BR	t o w | e r	v | v
VT | Cl	p r o w | e s s	v | v
VT | VT	c o u n t | d o w n	v c | c v

Syllable Type 4: Vowel Team (VT) ow (diphthong)

Sentences

Have students practice reading sentences for automaticity. These can also be used for dictation.

1. The cowhide belt is brown and white.
2. The rich pilot will endow his plane to the church.
3. Can we download the video onto the computer?
4. Trent spilled a heap of powder and did not sweep it up.
5. Whenever the man is out of town, he stays in a hotel.
6. Can you check to see if the clam chowder is fresh and hot?
7. The firm had to downsize to maintain a profit.
8. Maxwell hopes that his tennis prowess will lead to grand prizes.
9. Melvin takes the bus to go downtown; however, he prefers to ride the subway.
10. The cat gave a timid meow when the mastiff growled.
11. Petals from a safflower will stain fabric.
12. Maxwell's strong swing allows him to overpower his tennis opponents.

Syllable Type 4: Vowel Team (VT) igh

A syllable with this vowel team will be labeled VT.

Example: Decode: high|way (VT | VT; v | c v) Encode: h igh w ay

VT / VT high|way v | c v	VT / Cl bright|en v c | v
VT / VT night|light v c | c v	VT / Cl fright|en v c | v
Cl / VT flash|light v c | c v	O / VT de|light v | c v
VT / Cl high|ness v | c v	Cl / VT up|right v c | c v
O / VT twi|light v | c v	VT light|n(ing) *or*
Cl / VT spot|light v c | c v	VT light|ning v c | c v

Have students practice reading sentences for automaticity. These can also be used for dictation.

1. Did you use a flashlight at night?
2. Do not frighten the bat.
3. Can you put a spotlight on the deer?
4. I saw bright lightning flash at twilight.
5. I do not like the limelight.

Syllable Type 6: Consonant-le

Consonant-le occurs at the end of a word and is a syllable by itself. Although the final "e" is silent, there is an unwritten schwa sound that can be heard between the consonant and the "l." The c-le is circled, dividing the word into two syllables.

Example: Decode: siz | zle (Cl | C-le) Encode: s i z z l e

muz | zle (Cl | C-le)	ti | tle (O | C-le)	twid | dle (Cl | C-le)
puz | zle (Cl | C-le)	grid | dle (Cl | C-le)	pad | dle (Cl | C-le)
ket | tle (Cl | C-le)	no | ble (O | C-le)	ga | ble (O | C-le)
am | ple (Cl | C-le)	scru | ple (O | C-le)	bot | tle (Cl | C-le)
tod | dle (Cl | C-le)	fid | dle (Cl | C-le)	wig | gle (Cl | C-le)
la | dle (O | C-le)	muf | fle (Cl | C-le)	mid | dle (Cl | C-le)
gag | gle (Cl | C-le)	ma | ple (O | C-le)	pim | ple (Cl | C-le)
tat | tle (Cl | C-le)	sti | fle (O | C-le)	rum | ble (Cl | C-le)
siz | zle (Cl | C-le)	cod | dle (Cl | C-le)	ta | ble (O | C-le)
tum | ble (Cl | C-le)	noz | zle (Cl | C-le)	cat | tle (Cl | C-le)

Syllable Type 6: Consonant-le

Consonant-le occurs at the end of a word and is a syllable by itself. Although the final "e" is silent, there is an unwritten schwa sound that can be heard between the consonant and the "l." The c-le is circled, dividing the word into two syllables.

Cl | C-le

Example: Decode: s i z|z l e Encode: s i z z l e

O | C-le
c a|b l e

Cl | C-le
d r i z|z l e

O | C-le
f a|b l e

Cl | C-le
c a n|d l e

Cl | C-le
g a m|b l e

Cl | Cl | C-le
e x|a m|p l e
v c|v

Cl | Cl | C-le
e m|b e z|z l e
v c|c v

Cl | C-le
j u m|b l e

Cl | C-le
d i m|p l e

Cl | C-le
h u m|b l e

Cl | C-le
t e m|p l e

Cl | C-le
l i t|t l e

Cl | C-le
r a t|t l e

Cl | C-le
a p|p l e

Cl | Cl | C-le
r e a s|s e m b l e
v c|c v

O | O | C-le
f i|n a|g l e
v|c v

Cl | Cl | Cl | O | C-le
C o n|s t a n|t i n|o|p l e
v c| c v c|c v c|v

Cl | C-le
g e n|t l e n e s s

Cl C-le
u n t a n g l e

Syllable Type 6: Consonant-le

Sentences

Have students practice reading sentences for automaticity. These can also be used for dictation.

1. In no time, the light drizzle became mixed with thunder.
2. The clown can juggle sixteen apples, a dish, and a candle.
3. The accountant liked to wiggle in math class.
4. The little girl had a dimple on her cheek.
5. Do not giggle in class.
6. When the water is hot, the electric kettle will shut itself off.
7. The scoutmaster's bugle is on the table.
8. The proud little dog jumps over puddles to keep his feet clean.
9. Can you play the fiddle for the class?
10. Ask the teacher to provide an example of a fantastic essay.
11. Is it simple to assemble the purple table?
12. Can the player who fumbled the ball finagle the coach into allowing him to skip the huddle?
13. The fable was about a turtle and a rabbit.

Syllable Type 5: Bossy R (BR) ar

(also called r-controlled)

The "r" controls the vowel and produces an entirely new sound.

Example: Decode: car|pet (BR | Cl; v | c v) Encode: c a r p e t

car|bon (BR | Cl; v | c v)	gar|den (BR | Cl; v | c v)
gar|ment (BR | Cl; v | c v)	gar|net (BR | Cl; v | c v)
car|pet (BR | Cl; v | c v)	har|vest (BR | Cl; v | c v)
jar|gon (BR | Cl; v | c v)	kin|der|gar|ten (Cl | BR | BR | Cl; v c | c v | c v | c v)
mar|ket (BR | Cl; v | c v)	car|pet|bag|ger (BR | Cl | Cl | BR; v | c v c | c v c | c v)
par|don (BR | Cl; v | c v)	char|ter (BR | BR; v | c v)
Arc|tic (BR | Cl; v c | c v)	ar|cher (BR | BR; v | c v)

Syllable Type 5: Bossy R (BR) ar

(also called r-controlled)

The "r" controls the vowel and produces an entirely new sound.

Example: Decode: car|pet (BR | CI; v | c v) Encode: c a r p e t

par|snip (BR | CI; v c | c v)	gar|lic (BR | CI; v | c v)
dar|ling (BR; v | c v)	sar|cas|tic (BR | CI | CI; v | c v c | c v)
gar|ner (BR | BR; v | c v)	ar|ti|fact (BR | O | CI; v | c v | c v)
mar|lin (BR | CI; v | c v)	com|part|ment (CI | BR | CI; v c | c v c | c v)
par|lay (BR | VT; v | c v)	mar|ma|lade (BR | O | ME; v | c v | c v)
var|nish (BR | CI; v | c v)	ar|se|nic (BR | O | CI; v | c v | c v)
ar|dent (BR | CI; v | c v)	a|part|ment (O | BR | CI; v | c v c | c v)

Syllable Type 5: Bossy R (BR) ar

(also called r-controlled)

The "r" controls the vowel and produces an entirely new sound.

Example: Decode: car|pet (BR | Cl; v | c v)   Encode: c ar p e t

carpenter — car|pen|ter (BR | Cl | BR; v | c v c | c v)

lethargic — le|thar|gic (O | BR | Cl; v | c v | c v)

margin — mar|gin (BR | Cl; v | c v)

Syllable Type 5: Bossy R (BR) ar

Sentences

Have students practice reading sentences for automaticity. These can also be used for dictation.

1. Mix a dash of parsnip in the stuffing.
2. The Arctic wind made Arthur shiver.
3. Mark gave his darling wife a silver ring with a big garnet.
4. Will the candidate garner the votes he needs to defeat his opponent?
5. The farmer hopes to take a trip to fish for marlin.
6. Arthur will varnish the dull cart so that it will shine.
7. Coach Marcus is an ardent fan of the game of darts.
8. Marlene will charter a plane for her trip to the Arctic.
9. Chop the clove of garlic and roast it with the marlin.
10. Do not use a sarcastic tone when you speak to Marlene.
11. Artifacts from the Arctic will be on display at the art exhibit.
12. The bandit got a trunk with a compartment to hide the artifacts that he stole from the exhibit.
13. Margo will slather marmalade on her crisp toast.
14. Arthur felt too weak to clean his apartment.
15. A carpenter made cabinets for Arthur's apartment.
16. Marlene became a kindergarten teacher.

Syllable Type 5: Bossy R (BR) or

(also called r-controlled)

The "r" controls the vowel and produces an entirely new sound.

Example: Decode: tor|so (BR | O) Encode: t o r s o

ex|tort (Cl | BR)	men|tor (Cl | BR)
tor|so (BR | O)	or|deal (BR | VT)
dis|tort (Cl | BR)	es|cort (Cl | BR)
ex|port (Cl | BR)	tor|ment (BR | Cl)
or|bit (BR | Cl)	con|tort (Cl | BR)
vor|tex (BR | Cl)	for|lorn (BR | BR)
sor|did (BR | Cl)	bor|der (BR | BR)

Syllable Type 5: Bossy R (BR) or

(also called r-controlled)

The "r" controls the vowel and produces an entirely new sound.

Example: Decode: t o r | s o (BR | O; v | c v) Encode: t o r s o

BR | ME or | nate v | c v	BR | O | O tor | pe | do v | c v | c v
BR | O | ME or | ga | nize v | c v | c v	BR | O | Cl or | tho | dox v | c v | c v
BR | Cl | ME for | mu | late v | c v | c v	BR | O | Cl | Cl or | tho | don | tist v | c v | c v c | c v
BR | O | O tor | na | do v | c v | c v	Cl | BR | Cl im | por | tant v c | c v | c v
BR | Cl | O Or | lan | do v | c v c | c v	Cl | BR sup | port v c | c v
BR | O | ME por | cu | pine v | c v | c v	O | O | BR u | ni | form v | c v | c v
BR | Cl | Cl or | gan | ic v | c v c | v	Cl | BR | BR ex | plor | er v c | c v | v

Syllable Type 5: Bossy R (BR) or

(also called r-controlled)

The "r" controls the vowel and produces an entirely new sound.

Example: Decode: tor|so (BR | O; v | c v) Encode: t o r s o

dis|tort (Cl | BR; v c | c v)	land|lord (Cl | BR; v c | c v)
per|form (BR | BR; v | c v)	u|ni|corn (O | O | BR; v | c v | c v)
north|west (BR | Cl; v c | c v)	corn|meal (BR | VT; v c | c v)
pop|corn (Cl | BR; v c | c v)	

Syllable Type 5: Bossy R (BR) or

Sentences

Have students practice reading sentences for automaticity. These can also be used for dictation.

1. It is an ordeal for Arthur to clean his disgusting apartment.
2. The bailiff had to escort the witness from the stand.
3. The acrobat is so limber that she can twist her torso into the shape of a pretzel!
4. The rocket burst into orbit.
5. Do not torment your sister with that song!
6. A trade embargo will put a stop to what you can import or export.
7. The monster will whimper if he gets lost in the thunderstorm.
8. The storm will cross the border in the morning.
9. Will the garnet make the silver ring too ornate?
10. If you organize your locker, you may find the lunch that Mom packed for you.
11. The shipmates had to formulate a quick escape plan in case a torpedo hit the ship.
12. The stork hid in the basement of Arthur's apartment while the tornado was outside.

Syllable Type 5: Bossy R (BR) or

Sentences

Have students practice reading sentences for automaticity. These can also be used for dictation.

13. Will the hurricane hit Orlando?
14. If you step on a porcupine, it will hurt.
15. The explorer had the task of finding land for the people.
16. The farmer sells fresh, organic corn at the market.
17. The dentist informed Jordan that he must go to an orthodontist to fix his teeth.

Syllable Type 4: Vowel Team (VT) au

A syllable with this vowel team will be labeled VT.

Use "au" /aw/ in the beginning or middle of a word or syllable (e.g., August, vault). It also occasionally comes at the end of a syllable (e.g., caucus, saucy).

Example: Decode: pau | per (VT | BR) Encode: p au p er

nau | ti | lus (VT | O | Cl)	cau | cus (VT | Cl)
Aus | tin (VT | Cl)	laun | der (VT | BR)
Au | gust (VT | Cl)	Nas | sau (Cl | VT)
Au | to | mat (VT | O | Cl)	as | tro | naut (Cl | O | VT)
au | dit (VT | Cl)	laun | dry (VT | O)
gaunt | let (VT | Cl)	au | to | crat* (VT | O | Cl)
haunt | ed (/id/)	Mil | wau | kee (Cl | VT | VT)

*In this word, the "r" blend stays together because the word is divided by its Greek bases.

Syllable Type 4: Vowel Team (VT) au

A syllable with this vowel team will be labeled VT.

Use "au" /aw/ in the beginning or middle of a word or syllable (e.g., August, vault). It also occasionally comes at the end of a syllable (e.g., caucus, saucy).

VT | BR
Example: Decode: p a u | p e r   Encode: p a u p e r
v | c v

VT | CI
c a u s | t i c
v c | c v

VT | BR
s a u | c e r
v | c v

O | VT
d e | f r a u d
v | c v

VT | BR
p a u | p e r
v | c v

VT | CI | CI
a u | t h e n | t i c
v | c v c | c v

CI | VT
a p | p l a u d
v c | c v

VT | BR
a u | b u r n
v | c v

VT | BR | ME
c a u | t e r | i z e
v | c v | v

VT | O
s a u | c y
v | c v

Syllable Type 4: Vowel Team (VT) au

Sentences

Have students practice reading sentences for automaticity. These can also be used for dictation.

1. Put the cup of hot cocoa on the saucer.
2. The pauper cannot afford to get a raincoat.
3. Arthur never launders his sheets; even Arthur's dog will not sleep on the bed!
4. It is best not to use a caustic tone when speaking to an adult.
5. Applaud the actress for her excellent dramatic role.
6. The goddess has long, auburn locks and short bangs.
7. Saul will ask the astronaut for his autograph.
8. Launch the astronaut into outer space.
9. The teacher was born in Milwaukee, Wisconsin.
10. The man liked the authentic paintings in the art museum.
11. When the automatic gate got stuck, cars could not exit the parking lot.

Syllable Type 4: Vowel Team (VT) aw

A syllable with this vowel team will be labeled VT.

Use "aw" /aw/ at the end of a word or syllable or when followed by a single k, l, or n (e.g., saw, squawk, shawl, lawn). **Note:** The rules listed above are guidelines. However, some words do not follow these rules.

Example: Decode: jig | saw (Cl | VT; v c | c v) Encode: j i g s a w

with | draw (Cl | VT; v c | c v)	raw | hide (VT | ME; v | c v)
aw | ful (VT | Cl; v | c v)	draw | back (VT | Cl; v | c v)
jig | saw (Cl | VT; v c | c v)	out | law (VT | VT; v c | c v)
haw | thorn (VT | BR; v | c v)	mo | hawk (O | VT; v | c v)
saw | mill (VT | Cl; v | c v)	un | law | ful (Cl | VT | Cl; v c | c v | c v)
craw | fish (VT | Cl; v | c v)	out | law (VT | VT; v c | c v)

Syllable Type 4: Vowel Team (VT) aw

A syllable with this vowel team will be labeled VT.

Use "aw" /aw/ at the end of a word or syllable or when followed by a single k, l, or n (e.g., saw, squawk, shawl, lawn). **Note:** The rules listed above are guidelines. However, some words do not follow these rules.

Example: Decode: jig | saw (Cl | VT; v c | c v) Encode: j i g s a w

seesaw — VT | VT (see | saw; v | c v)

awning — VT | (aw | ning; v | c v)

guffaw — Cl | VT (guf | faw; v c | c v)

trawler — VT | BR (traw | ler; v | c v)

sawdust — VT | Cl (saw | dust; v | c v)

lockjaw — Cl | VT (lock | jaw; v c | c v)

mackinaw — Cl | O | VT (mack | i | naw; v c | v | c v)

Syllable Type 4: Vowel Team (VT) aw

Sentences

Have students practice reading sentences for automaticity. These can also be used for dictation.

1. In shop class, the students each made a jigsaw.
2. The pup got a splinter in his paw from playing in a pile of sawdust.
3. Stand under the awning until the hail stops pounding down.
4. We must stop at the bank and withdraw cash because the shop will not take credit cards.
5. The vet insists that eating rawhide can harm a dog.
6. Thorns from a hawthorn tree are sharp.
7. The candidate's guffaw was intended to mock his opponent.
8. There was a long line to play on the seesaw.
9. It is not safe to fish from a trawler in a storm.
10. Do not focus on the drawbacks of the job.
11. Stir the heap of prawns and crawfish into the gumbo.
12. The class did not wish to sing the silly, mawkish song.
13. Will a mackinaw and a scarf protect Alexander from the Arctic wind?

Y as a Vowel (ĭ)

"Y" says /ĭ/ in the middle of a word or syllable. These words are typically of Greek origin. When "y" is in the middle vowel position, it's considered a closed syllable.

Example: Decode: cyl | in | der (Cl | Cl | BR; vc | vc | c v) Encode: c y l i n d e r

gyp | sum (Cl | Cl)	sym | bol (Cl | Cl)
gym | nast (Cl | Cl)	E | gypt (O | Cl)
cyl | in | der (Cl | Cl | BR)	O | lym | pic (O | Cl | Cl)
syn | o | nym (Cl | O | Cl)	Syl | ves | ter (Cl | Cl | BR)
an | to | nym (Cl | O | Cl)	e | co | sys | tem (O | O | Cl | Cl)
gym | nas | tic (Cl | Cl | Cl)	syl | la | ble (Cl | O | C-le)
sys | tem (Cl | Cl)	sym | bol | ic (Cl | Cl | Cl)
mys | ter | y (Cl | BR | O)	syn | thet | ic (Cl | Cl | Cl)

Y as a Vowel (ĭ)

"Y" says /ĭ/ in the middle of a word or syllable. These words are typically of Greek origin. When "y" is in the middle vowel position, it's considered a closed syllable.

Example: Decode: cyl|in|der (Cl | Cl | BR; v c | v c | c v)   Encode: c y l i n d e r

analyst — an|al|yst (Cl | O | Cl)

cryptic — cryp|tic (Cl | Cl)

encrypted — en|crypt|ed (Cl | Cl | /id/)

crystal — crys|tal (Cl | Cl)

hypnotize — hyp|no|tize (Cl | O | ME)

mystify — mys|ti|fy (Cl | O | O)

syntax — syn|tax (Cl | Cl)

Y as a Vowel (ĭ)

Sentences

Have students practice reading sentences for automaticity. These can also be used for dictation.

1. If I ever go to a different continent, I would like to travel to Egypt.
2. We were unable to read the note because it was encrypted with a code.
3. Will the performer hypnotize people?
4. The gymnast is able to do many tricks on the high bars.
5. A can of green beans is shaped like a cylinder.
6. The Olympic athlete works with his coach to train all week long.
7. Sylvester lives down the street from my sister in Wisconsin.
8. The students know how to count and clap syllables.
9. The shirt is made from a soft, synthetic fabric.
10. Hot is an antonym for cold.
11. What is your teacher's system for turning in homework?
12. At first, I did not recognize the symbol on the round, gold coin.
13. The magic trick will mystify you.

Decoding with Digraph ph

Have students practice reading words with ph. Underline it as one unit.

Example: Decode: p h o | t o Encode: p h o t o

elephant	prophet
phoneme	pamphlet
photo	dolphin
alphabet	Memphis
Phillip	autograph*
telephone	phonograph*
photograph*	pictograph*

*In these words, the "r" blends stay together because the words are divided by their Greek bases.

Decoding with Digraph ph

Sentences

Have students practice reading sentences for automaticity. These can also be used for dictation.

1. Elvis got a banjo in Memphis.
2. The elephant was on the photo.
3. The old photo was thin.
4. Phillip had a pamphlet on the shelf.
5. The dolphin can swim fast.
6. I called my friend on the telephone yesterday morning.
7. Will we create a pictograph in math class today?
8. Irene would love to have an autograph from the music star.
9. How many letters are in the Greek alphabet?
10. The students will work with a new phoneme this week.
11. Did the old man have a phonograph to play music at the birthday party?

Decoding with ch (/k/ and /sh/)

When "ch" says /k/, the word is typically of Greek origin.

Example: Decode: chaos Encode: chaos

When "ch" says /sh/, the word is typically of French origin.

Example: Decode: chevron Encode: chevron

ch as /k/

chemist

technology

echo

mechanic

orchestra

monarch

architect

chaos

anarchy

arachnid

bronchitis

archive

ch as /sh/

Michigan

Charlene

Decoding with ch (/k/ and /sh/)

When "ch" says /k/, the word is typically of Greek origin.

Example: Decode: ch a | o s (O | CI; v | v) Encode: ch a o s

When "ch" says /sh/, the word is typically of French origin.

Example: Decode: ch e v | r o n (CI | CI; v c | c v) Encode: ch e v r o n

ch a p | e r | o ne (CI | BR | ME; v c | v | v)

ch a | r a de (O | ME; v | c v)

ch e v | r o n (CI | CI; v c | c v)

ch i f | f o n (CI | CI; v c | c v)

e ch | e | l o n (CI | O | CI; v c | v | c v)

ch a | gr i n* (O | CI; v | c v)

*** Please note:**
In this word, the "gr" blend stays together.

Decoding with ch (/k/ and /sh/)

Sentences

Have students practice reading sentences for automaticity. These can also be used for dictation.

ch as /k/

1. The chemist mixed the peroxide with the formula.
2. I need to take my car to a mechanic to get it fixed.
3. A spider is an arachnid.
4. When were you sick with bronchitis and the flu?
5. Stanly will find an architect to draw plans for the monument.
6. Technology helps us communicate with our friends and family.
7. Was there an echo when you were underground in the cave?
8. The monarch butterfly will go to Mexico to stay warm in the winter.
9. There was chaos in the crowd when the concert ended.

ch as /sh/

1. The students need a chaperone for the long trip.
2. The queen's coat had a chevron pattern.
3. My new dress is made of chiffon, velvet, and satin.
4. Charlene was shocked when she found out she finished in first place!

Decoding with /o͞o/ (spelled oo and ew)

The /o͞o/ sound can be spelled "oo" in the beginning, middle, or end of a word or syllable (e.g., ooze, scoop, shampoo).

Example: Decode: car|toon (BR | VT) Encode: c a r t o o n

The /o͞o/ sound is typically spelled "ew" at the end of a word (e.g., stew).

Example: Decode: out|grew (VT | VT) Encode: o u t g r e w

/o͞o/ spelled oo

car|toon (BR | VT)	poo|dle (VT | C-le)
af|ter|noon (Cl | BR | VT)	tooth|brush (VT | Cl)	mon|soon (Cl | VT)
class|room (Cl | VT)	sea|food (VT | VT)	pon|toon (Cl | VT)
soon|er (VT | BR)	noo|dle (VT | C-le)	rest|room (Cl | VT)
bath|room (Cl | VT)	boot|camp (VT | Cl)	re|boot (O | VT)
rac|coon (Cl | VT)	car|pool (BR | VT)	sham|poo (Cl | VT)
bam|boo (Cl | VT)	doo|dle (VT | C-le)	sound|proof (VT | VT)

Decoding with /o͞o/ (spelled oo and ew)

The /o͞o/ sound can be spelled "oo" in the beginning, middle, or end of a word or syllable (e.g., ooze, scoop, shampoo).

Example: Decode: car|toon (BR | VT; v c | c v) Encode: c a r t o o n

The /o͞o/ sound is typically spelled "ew" at the end of a word (e.g., stew).

Example: Decode: out|grew (VT | VT; v c | c v) Encode: o u t g r e w

mush|room (CI | VT; v c | c v)

tat|too (CI | VT; v c | c v)

tool|box (VT | CI; v c | c v)

mail|room (VT | VT; v c | c v)

room|mate (VT | ME; v c | c v)

/o͞o/ spelled ew

with|drew (CI | VT; v c | c v)

re|new (O | VT; v | c v)

cash|ew (CI | VT; v c | v)

crew|cut (VT | CI; v | c v)

new|born (VT | BR; v | c v)

out|grew (VT | VT; v c | c v)

un|screw (CI | VT; v c | c v)

Decoding with /o͞o/ (spelled oo and ew)

Sentences

Have students practice reading sentences for automaticity. These can also be used for dictation.

/o͞o/ spelled oo

1. Arlene and Shantel will go to the party this afternoon.
2. The actress screamed when the raccoon ran onto the set.
3. When eating seafood, do you prefer oysters, shrimp, or flounder?
4. Which cartoon does the little boy like the best?
5. We will carpool to save gas when we go to the concert.
6. The dog's shampoo smelled like flowers.
7. Have you checked the mailroom for the missing envelope?
8. We had to go inside because the barking poodle was so loud.
9. The band will record the music in a soundproof room.
10. The people had to flee from their homes because the monsoon dropped so much rain.
11. Sammy and Arnold love to take the pontoon on the lake in the summer.
12. The teacher had to reboot her computer when she was unable to access her files.

Decoding with /o͞o/ (spelled oo and ew)

Sentences

Have students practice reading sentences for automaticity. These can also be used for dictation.

/o͞o/ spelled ew

1. Andrew withdrew from the contest after he broke his arm.
2. The newborn was crying because she was hungry.
3. The elephant ate a cashew while at the zoo.
4. Bree quickly outgrew her pink shirt.
5. Help me unscrew the light bulb so we can put in a new one.
6. The boy's crewcut kept him cooler in the summer heat.
7. Will you renew your account at the bank?

Decoding with /o͝o/ (spelled oo and u)

/o͝o/ spelled "oo"

Example: Decode: f o o t | s t e p   Encode: f o o t s t e p

VT | Cl — v c | c v

/o͝o/ spelled "u"

Example: Decode: a m | b u s h   Encode: a m b u s h

Cl | Cl — v c | c v

*Be careful when dividing syllables with Bossy R. If there is a known blend, it may stay together. In addition, compound words are split between each smalle- word.

/o͝o/ spelled oo		
	goodness (VT | Cl; v | c v)	scrapbook (Cl | VT; v c | c v)
footnote (VT | ME; v c | c v)	textbook (Cl | VT; v c | c v)	precook (O | VT; v | c v)
wooden (VT | Cl; v c | v)	overlooked (O | BR | VT, /t/; v | c v | c v)	bookmark (VT | BR; v c | c v)
understood* (Cl | BR | VT; v c | c v | c v)	bookcase (VT | ME; v c | c v)	unhook (Cl | VT; v c | c v)
cook | ing	hardwood (BR | VT; v c | c v)	withstood (Cl | VT; v c | c v)
footstep (VT | Cl; v c | c v)	footprint (VT | Cl; v c | c v)	woodchuck (VT | Cl; v c | c v)

Decoding with /o͝o/ (spelled oo and u)

/o͝o/ spelled "oo"

Example: Decode: foot|step (VT | Cl; v c | c v) Encode: footstep

/o͝o/ spelled "u"

Example: Decode: am|bush (Cl | Cl; v c | c v) Encode: ambush

look|out (VT | VT; v c | v)

in|put (Cl | Cl; v c | c v)

hand|ful (Cl | Cl; v c | c v)

/o͝o/ spelled u

book|keep|er (VT | VT | BR; v c | c v c | v)

bull|doze (Cl | ME; v c | c v)

bush|es (/iz/)

am|bush (Cl | Cl; v c | c v)

push|o|ver (Cl | O | BR; v c | v | c v)

pull|ing

bull|frog (Cl | Cl; v c | c v)

Decoding with /o͝o/ (spelled oo and u)

Sentences

Have students practice reading sentences for automaticity. These can also be used for dictation.

/o͝o/ spelled oo

1. The footnote at the bottom of the page explained the point made by the witness.
2. What is Melvin cooking for dinner on Friday?
3. I am unable to locate my math textbook and class notes.
4. The footprint on the ground let us know that a fox had been in the woods.
5. My bookkeeper tells me when I should pay my taxes.
6. Be on the lookout for a new student in school this week.
7. Did you find the oak bookcase at the flea market?
8. We made a scrapbook to keep photographs of our friends.
9. When Arthur checked last night, the old, wooden box was still in the attic.
10. I must have overlooked the snake when I sprinted down the steps in a hurry to get to my car.

Decoding with /o͝o/ (spelled oo and u)

Sentences

Have students practice reading sentences for automaticity. These can also be used for dictation.

/o͝o/ spelled u

1. Did you provide your input for the project?
2. It felt like the bugs were trying to ambush me when I stepped into the woods.
3. I have a handful of candy to share with Jordan and Fernando.
4. The man in the truck will bulldoze the land so that it is flat.
5. Our team was pulling on the rope as hard as we could to try to win the contest.
6. Ashlee is a pushover for a cute puppy!

Other R-Controlled Combinations

/air/: ar, ear, er (bear)

Example: Decode: character Encode: character

/air/ spelled ar

parent

area

primary

parachute

necessary

character

Paris

January

apparently

vary

paragraph*

library**

legendary

wary

*In this word, the "r" blend stays together because it's divided by its Greek bases.

**The "br" blend stays together in this Latin word.

Other R-Controlled Combinations

/air/: ar, ear, er (bear)

Example: Decode: char|ac|ter (BR | Cl | BR; v | v c | c v) Encode: character

/air/ spelled ear	/air/ spelled er
bear|skin* (BR | Cl; v | c v)	fer|ret (BR | Cl; v | c v)
wear|ing	er|rand (BR | Cl; v | c v)
beach|wear (VT | BR; v c | c v)	fer|ry (BR | O; v | c v)
foot|wear (VT | BR; v c | c v)	mer|ry (BR | O; v | c v)
o|ver|bear|ing (O | BR | BR; v | c v | c v)	straw|ber|ry (VT | BR | O; v | c v | c v)
sleep|wear (VT | BR; v c | c v)	cran|ber|ry (Cl | BR | O; v c | c v | c v)

*The "sk" blend stays together in this compound word.

Other R-Controlled Combinations

/ar/: ear (heart)

Example: Decode: heart|burn (BR | BR; v c|c v) Encode: h ea r t b ur n

/ar/ spelled ear

heart|beat (BR | VT; v c|c v)

sweet|heart (VT | BR; v c|c v)

heart|burn (BR | BR; v c|c v)

Other R-Controlled Combinations

/er/: or, ar, ear, our (polar)

Example: Decode: calendar Encode: calendar

/er/ spelled or

network

worthless

workload

workshop

overworked (ed = /t/)

afterword

bookworm

schoolwork

reword

cantor

fervor

tractor

splendor

instructor

transistor

confessor

opportune

author

error

terror

/er/ spelled ar

polar

regular

popular

orchard

wizard

Other R-Controlled Combinations

/er/: or, ar, ear, our (polar)

Example: Decode: cal|en|dar (Cl | Cl | BR; vc | v c | c v) Encode: c a l e n d a r

	/er/ spelled ear	/er/ spelled our
liz|ard (Cl | BR; v c | v)		
cal|en|dar (Cl | Cl | BR; v c | v c | c v)	earth|worm (BR | BR; v c | c v)	jour|nal (BR | Cl; v | c v)
ce|dar (O | BR; v | c v)	learn|ing	cour|te|sy (BR | O | O; v | c v | c v)
bliz|zard (Cl | BR; v c | c v)	searched (/t/)	nour|ish (BR | Cl; v | v)
gram|mar (Cl | BR; v c | c v)	re|search (O | BR; v | c v)	
schol|ar (Cl | BR; v c | v)	ear|ly (BR | O; v | c v)	
mus|cu|lar (Cl | O | BR; v c | c v | c v)	earth|quake (BR | ME; v c | c v)	
bri|ar (O | BR; v | v)	earned (/d/)	
so|lar (O | BR; v | c v)	o|ver|heard (O | BR | BR; v | c v | c v)	

Other R-Controlled Combinations

/or/: ar, our (reward)

Example: Decode: quarter   Encode: quarter

/or/ spelled ar	/or/ spelled our	
toward	poured	
quarter	courtroom	
warning	mourning	
rewarded	courtyard	
awards	fourteen	
quartet	downpour	
warden	outpouring	
warthog		

Other R-Controlled Combinations

Sentences

Have students practice reading sentences for automaticity. These can also be used for dictation.

1. My parents live near the beach, and we take a trip to see them every year in August.
2. Albert's teacher said going to the library each week is necessary in order to get books to read.
3. It would be rude to ignore your sweetheart!
4. Apparently all the strawberry shakes have been devoured!
5. How will the quartet be able to sing with broken speakers?
6. The popular network is running a new sitcom this Friday night.
7. It takes teamwork to win a playoff game.
8. The mustard on the hamburger gave the man heartburn.
9. I felt the earthquake yesterday morning while I was sleeping.
10. When is the opportune moment to ask your darling to wed you?
11. It was pouring rain outside the courtroom.
12. Tigers and polar bears are carnivores.
13. Joseph should inquire about the exciting job opportunity.

Other R-Controlled Combinations

Sentences

Have students practice reading sentences for automaticity. These can also be used for dictation.

14. The character was wearing a different costume today than yesterday.
15. Is it necessary to wear a coat when it is super cold in January?
16. I picked a fresh apple from a nearby orchard.
17. Calvin's birthday party is on my calendar.
18. We could smell the cedar trees when we walked near them.
19. The muscular giant was kind and helpful.
20. Food will provide nourishment for your body.
21. The students are learning important facts from their schoolwork.
22. The chairman will get an award for treating his committee with respect.
23. Which shop sells beachwear and beach chairs?
24. Do not interfere while your parents are working.
25. Fran gave me a journal as a birthday gift.